Salama transports you to this part of the world through new, fresh and beautiful narratives far from the negative connotations often associated with it."   —Breanna Wilson, *Forbes*

"A thoughtful book that impresses with its sweeping history, evocative descriptions, and fascinating stories of people living along the river . . . An engaging travelogue for the 21st century and a reminder that the best travel isn't necessarily an epic adventure but a chance to hang out, getting to know new people—and yourself in the process."   —Erin Berger, *Outside*

STRANGER

IN THE

DESERT

ALSO BY JORDAN SALAMA

Every Day the River Changes

STRANGER

IN THE

DESERT

A FAMILY STORY

Jordan Salama

CATAPULT  NEW YORK

Stranger in the Desert

This is a work of nonfiction. However, some names and identifying details of individuals have been changed to protect their privacy, correspondence has been shortened for clarity, and dialogue has been reconstructed from memory.

Small portions of this book first appeared, in different forms, in essays published in *The New York Times* and *Tablet*.

First Catapult edition: 2024

ISBN: 978-1-64622-165-3

Library of Congress Control Number: 2023943193

Jacket design by Gregg Kulick
Jacket art of mountains of Argentina © Getty
Book design by Laura Berry

Catapult
New York, NY
books.catapult.co

Printed in the United States of America

1 3 5 7 9 10 8 6 4 2

For Abuela and Abuelo

Of course I don't believe it, but I like to tell these stories. I like it when they're told to me, and I would be sorry if they were lost. Besides, there's no guarantee that I haven't added something myself: maybe everyone who tells a story adds something, and that's how stories get started.

—PRIMO LEVI, "Lilith"

STRANGER

IN THE

DESERT

Map of Argentina, with author's route shown (hand-drawn, not to scale)

To: Moisés Salama
Subject: if you are curious

Hola Abuelo,

Here's the new book. It's not finished—I don't think
family stories ever are, not completely—but that's
okay. I've been writing it for so long, and it's taken so
many forms, that eventually I realized it was time to let
it rest for now. Still, I'm glad that I wrote down what I
did, even if only to make sure that I'll remember some
little details and moments from what's been a very
beautiful past few years of our lives. I hope you like it.

Jordan

PREFACE

Andes, 1922

UP IN THE PUNA, THE AIR WAS LIGHT AND COLD, the ground crumbly and dry. Everything was bleak where in the old days only the most hardened of herders and hunters lived—people who slept in adobe houses heated by fires burning across woodstoves, little pockets of warmth dotting these frigid and windy highlands of the Andes. In a waking dawn, a vicuña blinked, a condor soared, a salt flat glimmered in the distance; in a small house somewhere, a child was born without a father, and an old woman died dreaming of the sea.

At first light, the markets bustled as trading people began to exchange their goods: weathered clay pots and coca leaves, meats and fruits, jerkies and sweets, leathers and wools, clothes and home goods, old and new and everything in between. On mountainsides, day laborers descended into the mines, their weary faces darkened with soot from their daily pursuits of silver and nickel. In the fertile valleys, pickers and farmhands made their way through vineyards and cotton fields, and through orchards of walnut, olive, and citrus trees that were still and silent but for the occasional turbulence of a warm wind gusting down from the cordillera.

Horses sneered and mules whimpered as they faced the cold dawn of a new day's work. Gauchos stirred in their posts, tin kettles put to fire and gourds of hot mate passed around warm embers, the sound of last night's solitary guitar still echoing about the foothills and the canyons. Among the gauchos and scattered throughout the ranches that skirted even the farthest-reaching roads were a curious bunch of men who seemed, at first glance, very out of place. They spoke a foreign tongue—it wasn't Spanish, the language of the gauchos, who were also relative newcomers, displaced from their beloved Pampas; nor was it Aymara or Quechua, Diaguita or Huarpe, or any one of the other languages of the Indigenous peoples who had lived on the land for centuries but now found themselves increasingly attacked, conquered, and subjugated.

No: these curious men spoke Arabic, the language of Mesopotamia and the cradle of civilization, the language of the beginning of the world. Many of them had strange eating habits, like abstaining from any meat that they didn't already carry with them, salted and cured. Some of them did not travel on Saturdays, their day of rest. Others wrapped black cords around their arms, rocking back and forth as they rose from bed, and in this way they prayed. These men were different from most of the gauchos and the miners and the farmhands and the herders, yes, but with them they exchanged customs of the land they now shared—the mate and the card games and the folk songs—and the lands they only recently left behind.

It is said in the Andes that these people first came with the railroads, that their houses were near the train terminals in the cities where their wives and children lived, but their homes were on the road. And much like the famous traders of the old Silk Road, from whom they were descended, they brought everything with them as they traveled from town to town, carrying their goods for sale in little sacks over their shoulders, or in mule- and horse-drawn carts that clacked across the dirt trails and blistering sands.

Somehow these foreign traders made it everywhere, to what seemed like the farthest reaches of civilization—up dry, wintry mountain passes, and through river valleys that swelled with rain in the bountiful summers. They sold to anyone willing to give them something in return. The ranching families paid with silver, the lonely gauchos with coins, the farmers and the pickers with food, the wool sellers with ponchos, and the Indigenous people with ceramics from their adobe houses. In the chilly winters the stars were brilliant and numerous, though the sky looked different here in the Andes than it did in the northern countries where they came from. The moon here looked like it had been turned upside-down. But with time they would become used to the southern sky in Argentina, and their descendants would come to think nothing of it. Just as they and their children would eventually become Argentine, and just as their parents and grandparents had become Arabs before them, hundreds of years ago, in another life. In this new world, by the rivers and the valleys and the stars that guided them, the trading people found their way.

PART I

New York

2017

"KAN YA MAKAN . . ." IT HAPPENED, OR IT DIDN'T
happen; it was so, or it wasn't so. The Arabic phrase for "once
upon a time" always means a story is coming. What follows
can be as grand as a tale from *One Thousand and One Nights*—
the legendary Middle Eastern collection of fables in which the
vizier's daughter Scheherazade tells stories in order to save
herself from being killed—or as ordinary as a family legend
told across the kitchen table.

With *kan ya makan*, on my mother's side of the family,
stories have been passed down for many generations. My maternal grandmother, Mama Fortunée—whose Arabic name,
Mas'ouda, meant the same good fortune as it did in French—
said *kan ya makan* in America before launching into age-old
Iraqi children's rhymes, such as that of the bald-headed Jew
bullied in the souq, or the beetle who wore makeup and red
lipstick. So, too, did her great-grandmother before her—
Jummah, a woman so ancient that it was said she needed
three able-bodied men to help her walk across a room. On
winter nights in Baghdad, Jummah would summon her great-
grandchildren into a large bed heated by a charcoal brazier

under the covers to tell them stories of mischief and great adventure in the cradle of civilization. The terrifying legend of the jinni that haunted the mikveh, the Jewish ritual bath; the epics of Abu Zayd al-Hilali, whose exploits of war and conquest as a tribal leader in the Arabian desert made him a legendary hero of the pre-Islamic era. Jummah also told the story of her very own husband, Eliahou Rouben, a wealthy Jewish merchant in Baghdad. He began his career as a peddler who carried a sack over his shoulder and fended off thieves in the city streets. Eventually Eliahou Rouben built a trading empire—caravans of a thousand camels that plied the Silk Road—and would proudly display his battle scars from the early days as a measure of how far he'd come. But Eliahou Rouben's only son, from a prior marriage, was deemed unworthy of his father's wealthy inheritance because he had been born with six fingers on one hand. The legal battle that ensued after Eliahou Rouben's death exhausted the family fortune, forcing them to start anew, as they had had to do many times before.

The act of telling these stories from one generation to the next helped reinforce the idea that we were part of something larger than ourselves: that we had an identity that was worth preserving. Even though we no longer lived in Iraq anymore, we were still Iraqi Jews. We knew why we ululated at bar mitzvahs and why we hung amulets with garlic around newborns to ward off the evil eye. We knew why, at the end of Passover, we hit each other with green branches to usher in a new and bountiful spring. We knew why we spoke Arabic—though here I use the proverbial *we*, because, truth be told, for a long time *kan ya makan* were just about the only words in Arabic I knew. For reasons I would only come to understand years later, many in my family who spoke the language didn't want it passed down to us, their children and grandchildren. It was a language of trauma, of persecution, of exodus from the land where their ancestors had lived in peace for some two thousand years but had been expelled from, never to return, along with nearly one million other Jews in Arab lands. Yet Arabic, a poetic language rich with evocative recollections of lost worlds and forgotten existences, appeared everywhere in our lives in New York. I have vivid memories of family gatherings—of folding chairs set up around the edges of Long Island living rooms—where dozens of elderly relatives would sit, dinner plates in hand, jabbering away in the very language they wanted our family to forget. We were a true clan, and the fact that the clan gathered and jabbered and ate and drank afforded the very setting necessary for *kan ya makan*—for stories of the people who came before us, and their traditions, and their values—so that we would always remember we had a lineage, and a place within it.

On my father's side of the family, the side called Salama, I had never heard the phrase *kan ya makan* or the kinds of stories that followed it. I did not know the names of long-ago ancestors like Jummah or Eliahou Rouben. I felt somewhat guilty, even, that I could repeat next to nothing about their homelands or what they did with their lives. I was never quite sure why this absence existed. I knew so much more about one side of the family than the other—the other side also being Jewish, but from Syria and Argentina and many more places before and after that, too.

Perhaps this is because family origin stories so often surround singular, major events of migration or displacement.

Throughout history and around the world—from the steppes of Central Asia to the rivers of Mesopotamia to the highlands of South America—communities have told these origin stories in the form of folktales, oral histories, and religious creation myths. Indeed, for my Iraqi Jewish family, even more famous than the biblical Passover story of the prophet Moses leading the enslaved Israelites out of Egypt and into the desert was the retelling of the Babylonian exile of the sixth century B.C., when King Nebuchadnezzar expelled the Jews of the ancient kingdom of Judah to the land between the Tigris and the Euphrates. Some older family members could recount this tale with tears as fresh in their eyes as if they had gone through it themselves. When displacement is more recent, those newer voyages are sometimes the stories best remembered.

The little I did know about the Salamas, in broad strokes, was that the family has been, historically, almost perpetually on the move. The last name itself is suggestive, perhaps, of this transience: it means, at once, "hello," "goodbye," and "peace." I did not know what to make of this idea of setting down roots and creating community someplace only to have to pick up and move on to the next, but it happened in contexts large and small, and so the family story has been written anew with every migration.

When they were not compelled to migrate, nearly all my male ancestors worked as traveling salesmen. They were merchants who journeyed from town to town, by land and by sea, often along the great trade routes of the world. They sold tea and spices from horse-drawn carts and mule caravans; they balanced round trays of baklawa and other sweets for sale upon their heads in city streets; they carried burlap sacks filled with fabrics and clothes to rural provinces. They were movers of goods, but also of cultures and identities; their names and the languages they spoke carried traces of worlds lost and found, of places past.

Of the many branches of the Salama family that now exist in the world, the one I come from presently finds itself in New York. My grandparents—Abuelo and Abuela, Argentine transplants—settled in a large house on the crest of a hill in the woods near Peekskill, an hour's drive north of the city. We lived close, as did my father's two siblings, Victor and Daniella, and their children, my first cousins, Sebastian, Juliette, Liat, and Ilan. But other than this immediate family, there was hardly a larger "clan" around, ready-made for storytelling. We did not have extended family gatherings of a dozen great-aunts and great-uncles, of family friends from a synagogue, of cousins upon cousins. I hardly knew the names of those people, from those other branches, who'd ended up in Mexico City, Barcelona, Asunción, or Tel Aviv, or stayed in Buenos Aires.

Abuelo and Abuela's house was far from the Andes and Syria and Buenos Aires in some ways but very close in others. They lived in that house for more than forty years, and in all that time it hardly ever changed. Impeccably clean, with smooth floors and soft carpets, it is a home defined by a particular blend of places and memories and identities that cross continents and oceans, from Latin America to the Levant. For we are Jews, and we are Arabs, and we are Americans— Americans from the United States, but also Latin Americans. We are Arab Jews, and Arab Jews everywhere have had to become experts at trying to remember all that the world wishes for us to forget.

I do not want to forget: not my own experiences, nor the stories I heard of those who lived before me. I document everything, which is another way of saying that I live in fear of forgetting. I keep lists, in notebooks and on small scraps of paper stuffed in my pockets, of everyday things that I find compelling or beautiful: a café drenched in the sun; a shop filled with ticking clocks; a pair of dark, rotting wooden doors bursting with music. For a period while I was in college, I wrote down the title of every book I read and took note of particular songs I'd been listening to on repeat, so that in some distant future I might look back and conjure up the spaces I'd once inhabited, the feelings I'd felt during any particular moment in time. Writing about the world was a way of remembering my path through it. But in order to look within, I have found it necessary to go far, literally and figuratively. To ask questions of others in order to eventually, hopefully, find even the smallest reflections of myself. The thought that any life, for all of its beautiful details and complexities, can go so thoroughly unremembered fills me with dread. Those anxieties of forgetting—and the urge to go anywhere and everywhere—were transmitted to me through the generations of a uniquely mixed family background that no one else I knew seemed to share.

When I am someday very old and think back to Abuelo and Abuela's house, I will remember very specific things. I will remember that since the earliest days of my childhood, our family would gather there for lunch on Saturdays. Abuela would prepare chicken with linguini in red sauce, or baked empanadas, or Syrian meals of mujadara (rice with lentils, topped with caramelized onions) and kibbeh burghul (bulghur wheat patties lightly fried and stuffed with spiced meat and pine nuts) and white beans stewed in a rich tomato broth poured over rice. On summer afternoons we would set out a long table in the backyard while Abuelo grilled Argentine-style asados, smoke rising into the trees, trays stacked high with juicy cuts of meat and slices of watermelon, and mountain-sized bowls of salad tossed with olive oil and salt. We'd drink glasses of Diet Coke and red wine and with dessert we would sip our coffee from very small cups. When the day grew hot and long, and swarms of mosquitos descended upon our bare feet in the grass, we would rest the siesta on the couches and comfy armchairs in the many rooms of that large and warm house.

My abuelos were born and raised in Buenos Aires, but their ancestors came from elsewhere: Damascus, Aleppo, medieval Moorish Spain. On their shelves and in their cabinets, there were clues to that very motley lineage, if anyone cared to look. A tall, silver narghile—the type of water pipe used for smoking hookah—presided over the den, long out of use and weighed down with salt. It rested on the same shelf as old books, in a multitude of languages, that carried the musty smell of places past. An early edition of Bruce Chatwin's slender travelogue *In Patagonia*. Worn-out copies of Pío Baroja's restless novellas. Julio Cortázar's choose-your-own-adventure *Rayuela*; Jorge Luis Borges's time-bending *Ficciones*; a heavy, regal-looking printing of José Hernández's epic poem *The Gaucho Martín Fierro*; Jewish siddurim and a fading copy of the Quran. In the kitchen, hanging from the wall beside the table, were copper finjans for preparing Turkish coffee, large round pots for boiling pasta, and small cups for drinking mate, an herbal infusion that is the national drink of Argentina.

As a child, I was hardly aware that these things existed, let alone that each item held its own very particular significance. But now, maybe because of my time in the Andes, they are the first things I notice when I walk into a room. This was the same house, of course, where my grandparents spoke to my father and my aunt and uncle in Spanish peppered with Hebrew, and to each other in Spanish peppered with Arabic, and to me in English peppered with all the above. "Bye, mi rohi," Abuela still says to me before she hangs up the phone. Three words, three languages, three centuries and continents and existences. *Bye, my soul.*

I will remember that Abuela—whose name was Isabel Oss, nicknamed "China" (pronounced *cheena*, which comes from the Quechua word for "female")—often spoke with romantic turns of phrase like this. She said she took after her mother, a Damascus-born homemaker who spent afternoons in Buenos Aires frying onions in oil and listening to the radio, singing along to the poetic lyrics of Umm Kulthum, musical queen of the Arab world, whose melancholic orchestras reminded her of home. A lifetime later, Abuela would find herself doing the same in her kitchen in New York. Salad vegetables were rinsed, chopped, and tossed; onions were sautéed with turmeric and black pepper; dough was kneaded into thin patties; and water was put to a rolling boil to the Argentine tangos of Carlos Gardel and Aníbal Troilo, alongside those classic Arabic laments. The melodies filled the house, dancing in and out of the doorways and wrapping around the cabinets and chairs, the walls bursting with sound. Abuela seemed to know every lyric; they brought her back, she said, to the days of her childhood. She missed Buenos Aires with all of her heart. "Nostalgia is the most painful feeling in the world," she told me once, speaking loudly over the music at full volume, "so why can't I get enough of it?"

Abuelo, born in 1928 and fourteen years Abuela's senior, was always the more soft-spoken of the two. His name was Moisés Salama, but everyone called him "el Negro" since he was a boy because of the jet-black curls that set him apart from his fair-haired brothers and sisters. My grandparents were "China y Negro" to almost everyone who knew them. Their nicknames sometimes turned heads in the United States, but in Argentina, nicknames are as common (and crass) as "Rulo" (curly), "Bocha" (big-headed), or "Gordo" (fat).

My grandfather was hardly revealing when it came to himself or his past—only bits and pieces here and there—but then again, for a long time, I never asked. Quiet, calm, and fiercely independent, he kept a strict daily routine. He rose early, often with the first morning light, even on the grayest and coldest of winter days. He prepared a kettle of short-of-boiling water so that he and Abuela could share some mate. Abuela sipped first, because she took her mate sweet; Abuelo much preferred the pure, bitter, almost smoky taste of the yerba on his tongue. Their ritual was to drink at the kitchen table and read the news in their many languages from their many places—diarios *Clarín* and *La Nación*; *The Jerusalem Post*; *The New York Times*—while looking out the sliding glass door over the porch and the sprawling garden, still serene at this time of morning.

Once the day got going, Abuelo never stopped moving, not when there were carpentry projects to finish, and leaves to be raked, and a lawn to be mowed, and wooden birdhouses to be built, and plants to be tended to. All his life, he had been a person of many active pursuits in both work and leisure. For a time, as a student, he rowed crew on the great Río de la Plata, which draws the border between Argentina and Uruguay; before that, he tried competitive boxing, and before that he played soccer on the 1930s streets and sidewalks of Buenos Aires with a ball made from scraps of paper and muslin stockings. He ran the New York City marathon every year from his mid-sixties until his early eighties, when he was sidelined by a bout of pneumonia and valve-replacement surgery. In his nineties, he still did his daily stretches and walks.

A prominent member of the Argentine Socialist Party in the late 1950s and early '60s, he backpacked alongside other would-be revolutionaries in the Patagonian wilderness, camping beside glacial lakes, practicing military drills, and preparing for the day when the wave of leftist uprisings that were passing over Latin America would inevitably reach Argentina, too. He lived through four military coups in the first three and a half decades of his life in Buenos Aires, but the socialist revolution never arrived, and so, thirty-five, disillusioned, and in love, he and Abuela left for the United States.

Certainly, Abuelo didn't hesitate to get up and go whenever a patient would call, often interrupting his breakfast or lunch. He was a doctor—no small feat in the very traditional Argentine Syrian Jewish community of his time, where generation after generation of sons seemed to follow their fathers straight into shops and sales. Instead, as a young man, Abuelo studied medicine at the University of Buenos Aires, helping his family by hauling sacks of potatoes at dawn with his older brothers. He started his studies, though he didn't realize it at the time, in the same cohort as Ernesto Guevara de la Serna, who would later become known as "Che." This set him on a nearly seventy-year career course as a general practitioner: he opened his first clinic in the poor Buenos Aires suburb of Boulogne, just outside the city limits, where for a while his patients paid him in leather and eggs and live chickens, however they could. Several decades later, he would practice another kind of socialized medicine as the doctor of a communal Israeli kibbutz and the Arab villages that surrounded it. But first, after nearly being tempted to move to a very rural province out in the Pampas—the famous Argentine grasslands, where some distant family members had settled and their ranching town was in need of a doctor—he instead took a ship to New York, where he would eventually accept a full-time position at Coney Island Hospital in Brooklyn, and where a later move to the suburb of Peekskill would allow him to establish the small black-bag practice that he would maintain with rigor well into his old age.

By the time he was in his nineties, he worked only part-time. Patients rang the house and Abuela answered the phone.

"What time would you like to see the doctor, señora?" she asked, always in Spanish. "Yes, of course. Yes. He can meet you at five o'clock." Already she was gesturing to Abuelo, who would soon climb into his rickety 2000 Dodge Regency van filled with tango cassettes and race down the winding back roads to his office, the engine sputtering and spewing black exhaust.

"Nobody examines you from head to toe anymore like Abuelo does," Abuela explained one afternoon when I asked her why anyone would still see a ninety-three-year-old Argentine doctor who worked out of a small rented room in the back of a shopping center. Almost all of his patients were Latin American immigrants who had trouble accessing quality medical care in a language they could understand. "It's the next best thing to having a doctor in your own family. He can always go."

After seeing patients, after exercising, and after tending to his garden, most evenings Abuelo went down to his basement workshop, which was also a kind of museum. Down the carpeted staircase was a two-room, multipurpose space. On the right-hand side was an open area, a gallery of sorts. The wood-paneled walls were adorned with Abuelo's paintings and blown-up photographs of a young, now almost-unrecognizable family. A few of the paintings had duplicates, depicting similar scenes. There was one of an elderly, bearded Jewish man wearing a black hat and a suitcoat walking through an old neighborhood of cobblestone streets. Another, labeled "Caminito," had pastel-colored houses, and another showed a herd of horses running across the land. Several versions of these were hanging up or lying around, at different stages of creation, from pencil sketches to fully painted watercolors. It was as though the artist was gripped by a need to get them perfectly right.

As children, my cousins and I would play soccer on the hard gray carpet in that room, cringing when the ball rattled against the walls and made the frames shake. Sometimes a picture or a portrait would fall and Abuelo would come downstairs to find us there, guilty and ashamed, trying to hang it back up. He never said a word to us about that.

On the left-hand side of the basement was another, more cluttered room that we kids knew better than to disturb. At one end, a simple desk sat beneath wraparound bracket shelves filled with dozens of binders and boxes and books. One box was filled with stones, another held medical textbooks; yet another held a neatly organized pile of tango cassettes and VHS recordings of half a century of Argentina's World Cup soccer matches. The top shelf held a world-class collection of antique and international postage stamps. There were many maps: maps of Hudson Valley running trails, hiking maps from Patagonia, walking guides for Buenos Aires, and street schematics of the old cities of Damascus and Jerusalem. I remember one map pinned up in particular that showed bird migration patterns in the Americas. Highlighted among the rest of the migratory paths was that of Hazel, a peregrine falcon whose migration took her on a three-month journey from Baffin Island, at the northernmost reaches of our hemisphere, to Buenos Aires, the city of Abuelo's and Abuela's hearts.

We traveled to Argentina as a family only once before I turned eighteen. I was in high school during that trip, and with my father and my grandparents standing readily beside me, I barely had to speak Spanish. Because my mother came from Iraq at a young age, and because my father had also spent most of his life living in the United States, we only spoke English at home. And beyond soccer, I never felt a deep connection to Argentina. I did not understand the accent well, I didn't know my way around Buenos Aires, I drank mate only when invited. I never felt particularly Argentine myself. But on that trip, I understood for the first time just how deeply my abuelos did. Twelve hours on an airplane, and they changed completely. Abuelo and Abuela seemed to have been warmed by summertime in the country of their youth; there was a renewed energy about them. They held hands as they walked down the streets, which they knew by heart, for miles and miles. Abuelo brought his best-pressed button-down shirts, breast pockets stuffed with the telephone numbers and addresses of his many siblings and friends who still lived there.

One afternoon in Buenos Aires, we met one of Abuelo's older brothers for lunch. We sat in a large, old-style café, across dark-mahogany tables, and ate sweet pastries filled with dulce de leche. Tío Jacobo was an older spitting-image version of my grandfather—his stubble, his speaking cadence, even his breath smelled the same when I leaned in to give him a hug—except he knew hardly a word of English. Jacobo spoke gruffly and kindly and held my father's face in his thick hands as he repeatedly said how very happy he was to see him again after so many years. After we said farewell, we lingered on the sidewalk, and I turned back to catch a final glimpse of the old man hobbling off down the street back toward his apartment. I had never met someone like him before: someone whose presence felt so overwhelmingly familiar, but who existed in a world that until that week had been entirely imagined. In that moment I also sensed that he was someone I would probably never see again. I learned of his passing not long after returning to New York.

The greatest treasure my grandparents' basement held would change my life. One Thanksgiving, while I was in college, Abuela asked me to fetch several cartons of ice cream from the basement freezer, which sat next to Abuelo's library. The freezer was Abuela's domain, a stockpile of frozen homemade milanesas and fugazzettas, lahmajin, and kibbeh. As I opened the freezer door, one of Abuelo's binders caught my eye. It was labeled, on its spine, FAMILIA / EL CUENTO /

HISTORIA ANTIGUA (Family / The Story / Ancient History). Ice cream could wait. I closed the freezer door and pulled out the binder. It was by far the largest one on the shelf—a hulking, five-inch monster thick with life, stuffed with plastic sleeves and loose, yellowing papers and photographs falling out the bottom and the sides. I laid the thing carefully on the desk and opened it to the first page. Written in Spanish, this is how it began:

> *I'm not sure what it is that I'm about to write, but I've had this idea for a number of years now, ever since a conversation I had with my father when I turned thirteen and had my bar mitzvah . . .*

Clearly it was Abuelo's handwriting; I could tell by the very characteristically Argentine script, marked by irregular capitalization.

> *My father called me upstairs around sunset, after the religious ceremony and a small party that's always customary after a boy becomes a man. What my father said then has stuck with me ever since, burrowed away in a corner of my brain, and every now and then it crosses my mind. He began to tell me the ancient history . . .*

The next few pages went on to describe, in stunning detail, the story of our family's movements dating back more than five hundred years; it recorded an oral history passed down for something like a dozen generations, and this was almost

28 ➤ JORDAN SALAMA

certainly the first time such a story had ever been written down. The *Historia Antigua* spoke of the family's time in Spain during the medieval period, when the Islamic dynasties ruled and Sephardic Jews lived under the Umayyad and Abbasid empires. When in 1492 the Spanish monarchy issued the Alhambra Decree, forcing non-Catholics to either convert or flee, Abuelo wrote, "The majority of the family took boats, which cost a fortune, and disembarked in Rhodes, others in Salonika." In the *Historia Antigua*, I quickly learned, time moved in increments of centuries, not single years. "The family in Rhodes," it continued, "now reduced, eventually decided to go to the mainland of the Ottoman Empire, and established themselves in Smyrna. In Smyrna they lived for several centuries more, speaking old Judeo-Spanish (Ladino), for they never forgot about life in Spain. But little by little, they began spreading throughout the vast Turkish empire. Some went to Alexandria, others to Damascus, and others yet to Jerusalem and Jaffa."

They were marked not only by the name Salama, common across the Arab world, but also by a second surname, ibn Huedaie; its exact meaning was hardly agreed upon, but Abuelo thought it meant "son of Jews."

Abuelo wrote, now in the first person once more:

> *I come from the family that installed itself in Damascus. They spoke Arabic; the Ladino, which by that point no one understood, had been lost but for a few words. And the Hebrew, once spoken for so many centuries, was now only spoken during prayer, and they repeated it like parrots, and like parrots they did not understand what they were saying.*

At some point, almost all of the young male Jews began to leave the Ottoman Empire because religious minorities were being conscripted and sent to the army for many years. My father, Selim Salama, boarded a boat bound for Argentina. There he married my mother, Faride Cohen Hop, and had fourteen children, of whom eight survived past one year of life. The survivors were, in order of appearance: David, Amelia, Jacobo Alberto, Teresa, Jacobo Segundo, Hizel, Moisés (me), and Elías.

Astounded by my discovery, I began thumbing through the rest of the binder. It would take me months to eventually parse through it all and many more years to begin to understand everything that was harbored inside. If *National Geographic, Time,* or any other magazine to which Abuelo subscribed had ever published an article that mentioned a topic related to this history, let alone anyone named Salama, he'd included the snippet. Photographs, essays, and entire Wikipedia articles were printed in full. Letters of all kinds—from correspondences with old friends to typewritten form responses from magazine editors and politicians—dated back to the 1940s. Some family documents were from the nineteenth century.

It was a genizah of sorts, a trove of recollections, remembrance, and research. I had never before felt nostalgia for worlds I have never inhabited, or time periods I have never known, but that is how it was once I began my journey with Abuelo's special book. I didn't tell Abuelo that I'd discovered his papers. I assumed, since they had seemingly been kept secret for so long, that he didn't want me to see them. Instead, for several months following that very special Thanksgiving, I would look forward to school breaks and holidays at my grandparents' house, when I could quietly slip away from the crowd to go to the basement and read more of the *Historia Antigua*.

———

One afternoon at home in late December, Abuelo came into the kitchen and motioned for me to follow him. "I want to show you something," he told me.

He led me downstairs to the basement, and as we turned left toward his library, I saw that the *Historia Antigua* was already open on the desk. My face flushed. He knew. I was suddenly filled with a great deal of shame.

"You've been looking at my writing," Abuelo said. He always spoke so matter-of-factly in English, carefully choosing his words.

"Yes, I have," I said. "Abuelo, it's very interesting."

"Of course, it's very interesting, yes!" His face broke into a wide smile. He began to laugh as he spoke, and his eyes welled up with tears. "How much have you read?"

Nearly all of it. "Not much," I lied. I decided it was not the right moment to reveal that I had indeed reached a later section, three-quarters of the way through the binder, that described the intimate details of my grandfather's first handful of youthful romantic encounters.

"Very good, well, I have a question," he said, reaching not for the binder but for his laptop—a large, clunky old Windows machine that my brother periodically had to wipe clean of thousands of malware viruses that Abuelo accidentally downloaded while trying to watch soccer games from the pirated online streams of Argentine television channels.

"The printer," he continued, "it's not working."

He opened the computer, which lit up to reveal a lengthy, unsaved text document recently composed in the basic word-processing program WordPad. I recognized the small Courier font from other typewritten pages in the *Historia Antigua*.

"I would like to print this, okay, but the printer is not working," he repeated.

"It's because you're not connected to the internet, Abuelo." An easy fix. I clicked around, and in a few seconds, the printer hummed to life. Abuelo's eyes widened as two full pages of text emerged from the machine. "Oh, very good, thank you!" he said and promptly closed the nameless file. Before I could stop him, he clicked "Don't Save Changes" and placed the laptop in a desk drawer. He took the pages from the printer, slid them into a clear plastic binder sleeve, and clicked the metal rings closed. Another entry, filed. Satisfied, he stood up from his chair. "Let's go upstairs."

"Wait, Abuelo. You said you wanted to show me something."

"Ah!" He sat back down and thumbed through the binder—past a ketubah (a Jewish marriage contract) and photocopies of a faded booklet from the civil registry of Buenos Aires that contained the Spanish names and birthdates of his parents and each of his siblings—until he reached the pages we had just printed. "Read this."

I sat beside him.

The story was a description of his father—my great-grandfather, whose name, I had only recently learned, was

Selim Salama. Selim Salama, I thought, was a name that was not easy to forget.

> *Selim Salama was a very hardworking man, brawny but not tall. He was pure muscle from his constant activity. The rest of us never knew much about him because he never spoke about his personal life. He was strong and respected—or was he feared?*

I paused at a word I did not know.

"Abuelo, what is a hakham?" In Spanish it was spelled *jajam*, the *j*'s standing in for the guttural *h* common to Hebrew and Arabic.

"*Hakham*, in Judaism, means 'wise man,'" Abuelo said. "That's what we called the rabbi."

I nodded, and I continued reading:

> *Nearly everything I knew about my father was told to me by a friend of mine, the son of Rabbi Elías Suli from our synagogue Or Torah. My friend Jacobo, whom we called Jack, was older than me by two or three years. His father, Hakham Suli, urged him not to spend time with me because of my antireligious leanings (I was a socialist, and an atheist, since I was twelve years old). But Jack told me that Selim was very independent and hardly religious himself.*
>
> *Before I was born, my father's work as a traveling salesman involved riding a horse-drawn cart full of merchandise for sale in the towns in northern Argentina, eventually reaching Bolivia. He returned with*

ingots, solid bars of silver. Working and traveling in
this way, he slept where he could, he ate what was
available (not kosher, of course), and he relieved him-
self in open fields, or in village outposts and cesspits,
or along the road. He became accustomed to drinking
wine, and in the cities, he smoked Avanti cigars. At
home, he never used to drink wine . . .

I thought back to my mother's legendary merchant ancestor
from Iraq, with his supposed caravan of a thousand camels on
the Silk Road. Selim Salama seemed more real, more accessible
because of the generational proximity. Abuelo had known this
man, interacted with him—loved him, one would imagine.

"So your father was also a traveling salesman?" I asked.

But Abuelo looked puzzled by my question. He had
grown hard of hearing in the past few years, especially when
people spoke with him in English. I tried again in Spanish, a
language that I was still quite embarrassed to speak aloud, especially with him. "Entonces tu papá era vendedor ambulante
también?"

Now his face lit up again, like it had when I confessed I'd
been reading his stories. "Claro . . . todos!" he said in response
to my question. Everyone was, in those days. And for just
about the first time in my life, in Spanish, with the *Historia*
Antigua open beside us, Abuelo began to tell me a family story.

That yes, Selim Salama was yet another traveling salesman, and in the 1920s he traveled from town to town in a
horse-drawn cart filled with garments and textiles and other
materials for sale throughout the Andes mountains of northwest Argentina. He was a foreigner—more precisely, a Jewish

immigrant from Damascus who had fled to Argentina as a young adult around 1911 from the Ottoman Empire—and soon he found himself working alongside many of his compatriots, Jewish, Muslim, and Christian.

As a group, these immigrants—who hailed overwhelmingly from the Ottoman vilayets of Syria (Damascus), Beirut, and Aleppo, and the governorates of Mount Lebanon and Jerusalem—were often registered as turcos (Turks) by the Latin American immigration officials that received them because of their Ottoman origins. Particularly in Argentina, a country dominated at the time by Italian, German, and Russian migrations, it has more recently been suggested that this was more of an intentional reclassification than merely a simple mistake, part of a racialized effort to maintain the perception that the country's massive number of immigrants were mostly of European origin (in this case, Turkish instead of Arab), as reason enough to block other non-white migrants from entering the country. In any case, the misnomer stuck, and in some communities such a careless generalization of Syrian, Lebanese, Palestinian, and other Arabic-speaking immigrants—regardless of religion—has long carried a somewhat-offensive connotation.

But in Argentina, to be a turco, at least a Jewish one, has become a source of pride for many. "Co-turs," they call themselves, still today, in Argentine reverse slang. To be a turco means not only to be unique—to be hardy and strong, self-made and fiercely independent—but to recognize the people who worked tirelessly before you, and in turn to work tirelessly for those who will follow.

So, *kan ya makan*, for several weeks at a time and in classic turco fashion, Selim Salama would set off, largely alone, into the burning deserts, dizzying highlands, and isolated communities of the rugged Argentine countryside. Selim Salama began his journeys in the city of Mendoza, where he lived at the time with his wife and young children, and from there he proceeded along a northbound route of approximately one thousand miles. The Jew from Damascus passed through the provinces of Mendoza, San Juan, La Rioja, Catamarca, Salta, and Jujuy—from the fertile valleys to the breathtaking, inhospitable Andean plateau. This was Latin America's Wild West: a land of gauchos and runaways, of horses kicking up dust on long and lonely roads, of folk singers and dueling poets, rugged pastoralists and anyone else still angling for their place in an ever-changing world of modernization and globalization. Selim Salama claimed, among friends, to have made it all the way to southern Bolivia, a route regarded by historians to have been a three-month journey by pack animal. He would return home to Mendoza only after all was said and done, with his carriage empty but for a healthy quantity of silver to show for his sales.

Many years later, once back living in Buenos Aires and surrounded by old friends, Selim Salama would boast of his adventures in the mountains. They were almost always outlandish, occurring amid the harshest and most fantastic of backdrops. Jack Suli made sure to tell Abuelo whenever he heard one of these new stories—and Jack Suli was the rabbi's son, so he was to be believed. In one tale, Selim Salama and a traveling companion jumped from a train just before it plunged off the side of a mountain, killing everyone aboard; in another, Selim Salama fought off bandits who ambushed merchants along the remotest stretches of the route. Most often, though, Selim Salama boasted about how the trading men, far from their families and from the watchful eyes of tradition, found lovers along the road.

"The women wore long, flowing skirts without underwear." Twelve-year-old Jack Suli grinned when he told my grandfather the details of this particular story. "So they could please the traders passing by."

One day after school, Jack Suli told Abuelo that he'd overheard Selim Salama talking about children. Not the eight children he had with his wife, but other children—sons, more specifically—from his time in the Andes. That these lost sons were still out there somewhere.

Nothing more was ever said about the matter, but Abuelo did not forget this rumor, not ever in his life, not even after eighty years and three new languages and two new countries and three children and seven grandchildren of his own.

"Do you think what Jack Suli said is true?" I asked now.

"I don't know!" Abuelo was laughing again. "Maybe you can go look for them."

I couldn't tell if he was joking or not. "You can come with me," I said.

But Abuelo shook his head.

———

Winter turned to a restless spring. I began to read more pieces from the *Historia Antigua* with Abuelo by my side, so that he could explain the parts that I did not understand: the words and the phrases, the characters and the place-names. All my life we had spoken almost exclusively in English, but these conversations drifted increasingly into Spanish. Abuelo would say something in his native tongue, and I would respond in mine. We began to discuss matters of religion, of identity, of history; we drew and redrew family trees, and went over the names and backstories of ancestors long dead, as though they would be coming over for dinner at any moment. From the basement, I could open the binder to an entry—a photo, a letter—and travel to the narrow lanes of nineteenth-century Damascus, or the mean streets of 1930s Buenos Aires. Abuelo's entries about his own youth, his coming-of-age as a young man not much older than I was then, took me to the frozen hills of Patagonia, to the seashore of Mar del Plata, to the long and verdant pampas peppered with solitary ombú trees that had massive, far-reaching roots.

I couldn't shake the image I'd fashioned of Selim Salama and his horse-drawn cart, one hundred years earlier, trotting through the vast northwestern Andes. And I couldn't resist the idea that out there somewhere there could be long-lost descendants of his. I began a somewhat obsessive search online, filling my own folder with old newspaper clippings and historical articles from the early twentieth century that documented trading patterns in Argentina's rugged northwest toward the border with Bolivia. I made posts in niche Facebook groups across Argentina. I compared both of my grandparents' results from 23andMe, a genetic testing service, with the geographical movements outlined in the *Historia Antigua*. I took Abuelo's handwritten genealogy chart and input it into a website called Geni, a social network that allows users to create interactive ancestral maps and discover connections with others who have also constructed their own, with the goal of creating an ever-expanding global family tree.

I also created an email address for Abuelo so that I could send him some of these things. No one else knew about it except for me—I made sure of this to avoid spam and other distractions on the slow Windows computer that my grandfather hardly knew how to use. It was a one-way delivery service. I would send him something and then, if he found it interesting, he brought it up in conversation the next time we saw each other in person. The earliest messages I sent Abuelo were written in a Spanish so formal that it could have only been learned in American public school.

> Hola Abuelo,
>
> I made you an email for your computer. I will install it for you the next time we see each other. I will only send you things for the family history project. I'll start with the family tree that I showed you yesterday.
>
> I hope that you're staying well. See you soon.
>
> Abrazos,
> Jordan

As I grew my own collection of materials, I wondered what it might look like if I traveled to Argentina and followed in my great-grandfather's footsteps to look for the places and people he might have left behind. I reached out to extended family members, some of them for the very first time. First, I called Abuelo's two living siblings, asking after more information, and both seemed less than pleased with my desire to go searching for their father's other children in the Andes.

"Nooo!" my 102-year-old great-aunt Teresa exclaimed from Barcelona at the suggestion that her father could have done something so scandalous. "Never, never, never!"

From Miami, my ninety-year-old great-uncle Elías also doubted this to be true, though he had heard the rumors. He also mentioned that he'd once caught a glimpse of a small notebook that belonged to his father and contained his business accounts from his time in the Argentine northwest— scribbles of names and numerals that would have surely led me in the right direction. My eyes widened before he told me that the notebook was long gone now.

If in his life he was known for his brute strength and formidable countenance, in the many years since his death in 1960, Selim Salama had developed a polarizing reputation among his descendants—both among those who were old enough to personally remember the man, and among those who were too young to ever have known him at all. Selim Salama was a man who by all accounts beat his male children cruelly and relentlessly. "My father was brutal," Abuelo told me bluntly. "He gave us tremendous poundings." Sometimes it was on the backside with a belt; more often it was with a stick on the soles of their feet. His children could give no excuse to avoid the violence. He would beat his sons anytime they would come home without a peso to show for that day's work. He would beat them whenever they would skip Hebrew school to play soccer in the streets or to watch Boca Juniors at the stadium down the block.

In his own way, he also fiercely defended his children

against the violence of others. "My elementary school, the Bernardo de Irigoyen Primary School for Boys, was run by a wicked headmaster named Miguel Chimento," Abuelo read aloud one afternoon from the *Historia Antigua* in Spanish. "One morning, after I was late to school, the headmaster slapped me in his office." Sobbing, Abuelo ran home to his father, who promptly walked with him back to the school and grabbed the headmaster by the collar of his shirt. "I am the only one to lay a hand on my son," Selim Salama said, as he was restrained by several other men.

There is a phenomenon that seems common among families like ours, families that have not too long ago come from somewhere else. The first generation is wary of, and perhaps even outright averse to, learning the details of the lives of their parents. "When we were girls in Buenos Aires, my sisters and I would sit far away from our father on the bus," Abuela told me once, "just so that he wouldn't speak Arabic to us in public. I remember wanting to die of shame whenever he opened his mouth. How stupid I was . . ."

The next generations, however, are far more likely to want to understand, to discover, and to reclaim. In this way, a bombastic bunch of my father's older cousins—Selim Salama's grandchildren, who in late middle age were now scattered about the Americas—took a great interest in what I was trying to find. There was Hector "Coco" Salama, a respected clinical psychologist who lived just a few blocks from a university he founded decades ago in Mexico City; Betty Salama, a shop owner, and Marcos "Rulo" Bamballi Salama, an architect with curly white hair and a gray mustache, who lived in Buenos Aires; Jorge Salama, who had migrated to the Paraguayan capital; and many others. They recalled, perhaps more fondly through the forgiving eyes of childhood, their grandparents Selim and Faride taking them to the lakeside town of Caruhé, whose salty waters were thought to have restorative skincare benefits; they remembered sitting beside their grandparents' knees at night and hearing them speak in Arabic when they did not want the children to understand.

"My grandfather was a storyteller," Coco told me on the phone one afternoon, from his home in Mexico. "This will be a great adventure."

My idea was to travel by myself, but it became clear that I would not be making this journey entirely alone. Abuelo, too, was a storyteller, and he was steadfast in his belief in my project. He'd had a complicated relationship with his father and always wondered if there was more to the old man than he knew. "Habrá que ver . . ." Abuelo would say about various things, even though he would be staying home. *We'll have to see.*

"We'll have to see if my friend Doctor Adolfo Yunis still lives in Buenos Aires."

"We'll have to see if my father appears in any of the registries up north."

"We'll have to see if we find one of Selim's missing descendants."

As summer approached, I began making concrete plans. I purchased a fold-up *National Geographic* road map of Argentina. After Passover seder, I spread it out on the basement table to show Abuelo my plotted route up the cordillera, circling cities and towns with a pen as I went. I would journey by land through seven distinct provinces. Like my great-grandfather, I would begin in Mendoza, and if all went well, I would end up in southern Bolivia after a few weeks' time. And I would go in search of these unknown relatives, whom I'd begun to call the "Lost Salamas."

For all the excitement, in the days leading up to my departure, I began to have doubts, too. Did any of this make sense? I would trade summer in New York for winter in Argentina. My grandparents were getting older. Going would mean leaving my family here in search of family I wasn't even sure existed, in a country where I did not feel I belonged. At times, I also wondered if I was following in the footsteps of a madman. But if I'd learned anything coming from a family shaped by forced migrations, I understood that any opportunity to travel by choice was a privilege, and that such journeys should be taken with purpose and meaning. I knew that the only way to begin to understand our wandering family was to hit the road.

What exactly I wanted to glean from encounters with any long-lost relatives scattered about the Argentine highlands was less clear to me. But I was interested in telling stories, and there seemed to be a story here. I was a college student when I found the *Historia Antigua*, and although I hadn't the slightest idea what I wanted to do with my life practically speaking, I'd grown interested in Latin American literature, Middle Eastern folklore, and Jewish history. Not much was written in English on those topics together. There were academic texts, yes, but for all the theory and sociopolitical analysis, there seemed very little in the way of portraits of how regular people lived. Our stories were very rarely on the shelves in the libraries of Jewish literature. The *Historia Antigua* quite literally was, though, and in it I found a realm in which my many identities existed more in harmony than in conflict. It arrived at a time in my life when I was constantly asking questions of the world, trying to find my place. Maybe, I thought, a journey up the spine of the Americas could help me figure it out.

"Abuelo," I said one evening, right before I left for Argentina, "I'm nervous."

He looked hard at me, raising his eyebrows and widening his eyes. Behind him the low golden light of the sun streamed in through the small basement window and illuminated his books, his paintings, his handcrafted wooden ships, a lifetime of adventures.

"Don't be," Abuelo said. "You'll be fine, so long as you remember one thing and one thing only: feeling like you don't fully belong anywhere probably means that you belong a little bit everywhere."

Buenos Aires

I LANDED IN BUENOS AIRES ON A RAINY DAY IN July. It was midwinter in the southern hemisphere, but the air was unseasonably warm. My "uncle" Nestor picked me up at the airport—to others I referred to him as my uncle, un tío, but in fact he was my father's first cousin. Nestor's father, Hizel, died a year earlier and was one of Abuelo's older siblings I would never meet.

Nestor had a kind, round face and gentle eyes. He also happened to be one of the people I love most in this world: a romantic Argentine to his core, of the type who sends three-minute-long WhatsApp voice memos just to send regards and who often speaks with the exaggerated, melodramatic gusto of an opera singer. And like most Syrian Argentine Jews whose ancestors were traveling salesmen, he worked as a shopkeeper, selling undergarments from a small store in a suburb of Buenos Aires. Nestor greeted me with a long and warm hug, holding my cheek in his hand as he asked me how I was. We loaded my bags into his small gray Chevrolet and set off toward the city center.

We passed warehouses, pastures, and the training complex for the Argentine national soccer team before descending

into a labyrinth of darkened city streets. He drove remarkably, painfully slowly. I wondered if this was because he had
something he wanted to tell me before we got to his house. I
told him of my plans to head west to Mendoza in a few days,
and from there to make my way north, by land, to Bolivia. A
great deal of people had eagerly helped me plan the route, I
continued: historians from American and Argentine universities, leaders from local Jewish communities spanning several
continents, and old friends of my grandfather's whose phone
numbers I'd gleaned from scraps of paper scattered throughout the *Historia Antigua*. As a way of proving that I was serious, I showed him the shiny Bolivian visa that had been
stamped into my passport by a diplomat at the country's New
York City consulate.

"Really, I'm not sure I understand what it is you're looking
for," Nestor confessed.

The Lost Salamas, I reminded him.

"The Lost Salamas!" Nestor burst out laughing. "Escuchá,
listen, querido, my grandfather, your great-grandfather, he
was a total harta. Do you know what *harta* means?" I didn't.
Nestor said the word with a long, breathy *h* at the beginning.
It was Arabic, he explained, "for someone completely full of
shit."

Nestor's wife, Corina, and their teenage children, Dana
and Martín, greeted us when we walked in the door of their
house in the leafy, middle-class Buenos Aires neighborhood
of Caballito. "Welcome home, Jordan!" Corina said, wrapping
me in a long hug. Their black-and-beige cat, Reina, nipped at
my socks. When Corina pronounced my name, she replaced
the *J* with a long *sh* sound; almost everyone I would meet in

Argentina did this. In Buenos Aires, I was not Jordan but *Shorthan.*

I was to sleep in Martín's room, while he slept on an air mattress on the floor in his older sister's room next door. I protested, offering to take the floor myself, but the family insisted. Martín's bed was small. My feet dangled off the edge if I didn't bring my knees up toward my stomach, curled up in a ball. That first night, restless with anticipation for what was to come and distracted by the new sounds of an unfamiliar city—the roar of the motorcycles and the diesel buses and the barking of street dogs—I put myself to sleep with music in my earbuds and had vivid dreams of the Andes. I dreamt that I was in a lunar, desert-like landscape where the wind blew hard and cold and where nobody knew my name. Even I couldn't remember it if I tried. There were people and pack animals in caravans all around me. The people I dreamt about spoke the same mix of Arabic and Spanish that Nestor did. It sounded fluid, like it was one single language and not a mix of two or three. That so much of Arabic is so easily Hispanicized is not surprising. The Muslim conquests in the Middle Ages, which brought the reign of the Arab Umayyad Caliphate to the Iberian Peninsula, gifted the Spanish language thousands of words and phrases with Semitic roots. Words like *aceituna* (olive) and *ajedrez* (chess) in Spanish have Arabic etymologies—*zeytun* and *shatranj.* Expressions like *ojalá* (hopefully) invoke the name of Allah, God, in the same way that Arabic speakers do when they say *alhamdullilah* (praise God) or *inshallah* (God willing) or *allah ma'akon* (God be with you), often regardless of their religion.

Like so much that was soon to come in the countryside,

this new blended speech was at once familiar and unfamiliar to me. Suddenly I had to practically employ these languages and dialects in contexts where I could not resort to English. My Spanish was conversational, but I was far from the level of a native speaker and my American accent was strong; I stumbled over pronouns and struggled to express specific concepts that I had until then only ever thought about in English. My Arabic, of course, was nonexistent—I knew that someday I wanted to learn the other language that I'd heard in passing all my life, but at that point, Spanish was enough of an uphill battle. I found, though, that when people injected Arabic words into Spanish conversation, I better intuited the overall meaning of what they were saying.

Everything was a challenge, from answering Corina's questions while brushing my teeth first thing in the morning to thinking quickly on the soccer field with Dana and Martín. In the evenings, we played backgammon and watched episodes of *Fauda*, an Israeli spy thriller series, with characters speaking a mix of Hebrew and Arabic. The Hebrew speakers and the Arabic speakers were largely enemies on-screen, but my cousins and I couldn't help but point out all the things that were familiar to us: the same sweets that our grandmothers made, the music and dancing that we recognized, the words here and there, in both languages, that we understood. The Spanish subtitles made for an additional test. By the end of most nights, I was so tired from translating all these many languages in my head that I didn't want to say another word.

———

To: Moisés Salama
Subject: MAPA DAMASCO

Hola Abuelo,

Today was my first day in Buenos Aires. I'm with Nestor and his family, who are taking good care of me. They're all doing well and they wish you and Abuela were here with us.

I wanted to share something with you. Not long ago, someone sent me a picture of a hand-drawn map of the old Jewish quarter of Damascus, made by a Syrian man in Mexico named Michael Romano Karake. On Facebook, I found his daughter, Sarita, and today she sent me this digital version. You can see many of the last names of people in our family. It looks like they were all neighbors. Let me know what you think.

Saludos,
Jordan

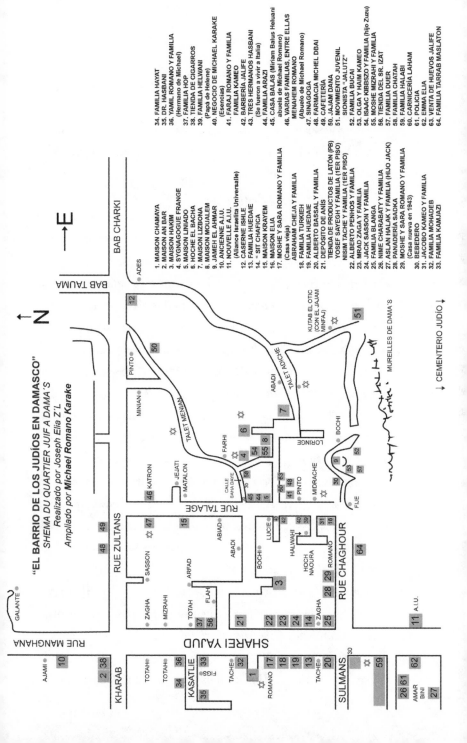

"EL BARRIO DE LOS JUDÍOS EN DAMASCO"
SHEMA DU QUARTIER JUIF A DAMA'S
Realizado por Joseph Elia Z'L
Ampliado por Michael Romano Karake

N ←

E →

BAB TAUMA

BAB CHARKI

1. MAISON CHAMAYA
2. MAISON AN BAR
3. MAISON HAKIM
4. SYGNAGOGUE FRANGE
5. MAISON LINIADO
6. HOCHE EL BACHA
7. MAISON LIZBONA
8. MAISON MOUALEM
9. JAMEH EL AHMAR
10. ANCIENNE A.I.U.
11. NOUVELLE A.I.U.
   (Aliance Israelita Universalle)
12. CASERNE ISHLE
13. FAMILIA HUEDAIE
14. " SIT CHAFICA
15. MAISON KRAYEM
16. MAISON ELIA
17. MOSHE Y SARA ROMANO Y FAMILIA
   (Casa vieja)
   ABRAHAM CHEJA Y FAMILIA
18. FAMILIA HUEDAIE
19. FAMILIA TURKIEH
20. ALBERTO BASSAL Y FAMILIA
21. DEPÓSITO DE ANÍS
   TIENDA DE PRODUCTOS DE LATÓN (PB)
   YOSEF SAYEGH Y FAMILIA (1ER PISO)
   NISIM TACHE Y FAMILIA (1ER PISO)
22. ALBERTO PENHOS Y FAMILIA
23. MRAD ZAGA Y FAMILIA
24. JACK SASSON Y FAMILIA
25. FAMILIA BLANGA
26. NIME CHARABATY Y FAMILIA
27. ASLAN HALAK Y FAMILIA (HIJO JACK)
28. PANADERIA SADKA
29. MOSHE Y SARA ROMANO Y FAMILIA
   (Casa nueva en 1943)
30. BEBEDERO
31. JACOBO KAMEO Y FAMILIA
32. FAMILIA MOHADEB
33. FAMILIA KAMJAZI

34. FAMILIA HAYAT
35. DR. HASBANI
36. YAMIL ROMANO Y FAMILIA
   (Hermano de Michael)
37. FAMILIA HOP
38. TIENDA DE CIGARROS
39. FAMILIA HELWANI
   (Papá de Helene)
40. NEGOCIO DE MICHAEL KARAKE
   (Esencias)
41. FARAJ ROMANO Y FAMILIA
   FAMILIA KAMEO
42. BARBERÍA JALIFE
43. TRES HERMANOS HASBANI
   (Se fueron a vivir a Italia)
44. FAMILIA ARAZI
45. CASA BALAS (Miriam Balus Heluani
   abuela de Michael Romano)
46. VARIAS FAMILIAS, ENTRE ELLAS
   MENAHEM ROMANO
   (Abuelo de Michael Romano)
47. SINAGOGA
48. FARMACIA MICHEL DBAI
49. CAFETERÍA
50. JAJAM DANA
51. MOVIMIENTO JUVENIL
   SIONISTA "JALUTZ"
52. FAMILIA BUCAI
53. OLGA Y HAIM KAMEO
54. ISAAC KIBBSZO Y FAMILIA (hijo Zuzu)
55. MOSHE MIZRAHI Y FAMILIA
56. TIENDA DEL SR. IZAT
57. FAMILIA DUER
58. FAMILIA CHATAH
59. FAMILIA HALABI
60. CARNICERÍA LAHAM
61. POLICIA
62. EMMA ELIA
63. VENTA DE HUEVOS JALIFE
64. FAMILIA TARRAB MASLATON

← CEMENTERIO JUDÍO

MURELLES DE DAMA'S

RUE MANGHANA
RUE ZULTANS
RUE TALAGE
RUE CHAGHOUR
SHAREI YAUD
SULMANS
KHARAB
KASATLIE

GALANTE
AJAMI
TOTAH
TOTAH
TACHE
TACHE
ROMANO
ZAGHA
MIZRAHI
TOTAH
FLAH
ABIAD
ABIAD
SASSON
KATRON
MINIAN
PINTO
FARHI
JEJATI
MATALON
LUCIE
BOCHI
ARFAD
HALWAHI
HOCH NAOURA
ZAGHA
ROMANO
CALLE SAHA DAVE
TALET MENIAN
TALET ADICHE
LORINGE
BOCHI
MIDRACHE
PINTO
FJE
ADES
KUTAB EL OTIC
(CON EL JAJAM MINFAJ)
FIGS
AMAR BINI

Historia Antigua

Damascus

My father was born in Damascus, Syria—when it was a province of the Ottoman Empire—around 1886. He never knew exactly the year, nor did he care.

The Salama clan—or the Salama ibn Huedaie clan, as they were long known in order to distinguish themselves from the Muslims and Christians in the city who shared the common surname— lived in the heart of the Haret al-Yahud, Damascus's old Jewish quarter. Bab Sharqi, one of the many ancient gates to the city, marked the most prominent entrance to this area, a crossroads of history and faiths. Just to the north of the Haret al-Yahud were numerous Catholic churches; to the west stood the great Umayyad Mosque, with its grand courtyard and epic interior archways and many tall minarets. In the narrow-alleyed souqs, fruit and nuts from the surrounding orchards were sold from straw baskets and wooden bins—because in those days, the Haret al-Yahud sat at the edge of one of the great oases of the Levant, where verdant trees bore apricots and mulberries and walnuts, pears and peaches and plums. The fruit sellers worked beside the glass blowers and the coppersmiths, the bakers and the butchers, while the passing Silk Road traders hawked Turkish spices and Persian rugs and wool from the Central Asian steppes.

Jews have been present within the borders of modern-day Syria since at least the first century, when some ten thousand of them lived in Damascus. Some situate the community's founding even further back, around 1000 B.C., under the rule of King David during biblical times. This ancient community of Jews is among the oldest in the world, along with others indigenous across the Middle East and North Africa for millennia. They were called Musta'arabi Jews, which literally means "like Arabs." After the 1492 Alhambra Decree, the edict from the Catholic monarchs of Spain that led to the expulsion of non-Catholics from the Iberian Peninsula, tens of thousands of practicing Sephardic (Spanish) Jews and their descendants joined these Middle Eastern and North African Jews, in large part adopting their customs over the following centuries. Such was the case in Damascus, which was under the rule of the Ottoman Empire from 1516, and whose various religious minorities were known as dhimmis by the Muslim sultans. The dhimmis paid higher taxes because they were not Muslim. Their churches and synagogues couldn't be tall and prominent, they had to ride donkeys instead of horses, and they were prevented from bearing arms. Despite their dhimmi status, the small Jewish community of Damascus lived, for a long while, in relative peace. And so the Haret al-Yahud hosted a small but thriving center of Jewish life—a blend of cultures, marked by surnames including Romano (from Rome), Lisbona (from Lisbon), and Turkieh (from Turkey); Halabi (from Aleppo), Chami (from Damascus), and Mizrahi (from the East).

In the Haret al-Yahud, there were spacious palaces—featuring multiple courtyards and fountains and secret passageways enjoyed by wealthy families—as well as tenement-style quarters, large homes where sometimes thirty or more families rented the individual bedrooms and shared the common kitchen and bathroom areas. Nearly all of the houses had interior plant-filled courtyards, and the streets of the quarter were so narrow that the second-floor bay windows nearly touched one another above the maze of public lanes. At night, when a cool breeze came down from the nearby mountains, parents and children slept out on the cool roofs under the stars. There were numerous synagogues—the Alfaranj and the Minyan within the city gates, and the ancient Eliahu Hanavi synagogue complex in the nearby district of Jobar, built atop a cave famously said to have been the refuge of the prophet Elijah. There were Jewish schools, like the Ben Maimon and the French-funded Alliance Israélite Universelle, which gave the Arabic-speaking Jews exposure to the Latin alphabet.

It is a world that no longer exists. When my father was born, there were some twenty-five thousand Jews in the Ottoman province of Syria, split evenly between its two most important cities, Damascus and Aleppo. Today, twelve elderly Jews persist in Damascus; none remain in Aleppo.

But back then, in the neighborhood, nearly everyone knew one another. The Salama Huedaie family lived near the families Penhos, Cohen Hop, Zagha, and Amar; perhaps it wasn't a coincidence, then, that years later, the children and grandchildren of some of those clans would marry in new countries around the world.

Damascus was always a working-class city, and its Jews were hardly an exception. But during the second half of the nineteenth century, the city went through hard times economically. The 1869 completion of the Suez Canal shifted global trade routes and quickened the decline of the old Silk Road and the landlocked population centers (such as Damascus and Aleppo) it served. The glory days of land-trading caravans, of pack animals traversing desert, mountains, and steppe, were quickly vanishing. Life soon became very difficult for people across the Levant. There was rampant hunger and poverty. Many families rarely ate meat on occasions other than festivals or Shabbat.

This first migratory wave out of Ottoman Syria was

overwhelmingly an economic migration. A large number of Jew-
ish migrants followed the cotton trade all the way to Manchester,
England. Many others established businesses in New York, es-
pecially on the Lower East Side, where they lived alongside the
Eastern European Jews and non-Jewish Italian and Russian and
Polish immigrants who more famously filled the tenements of that
dangerously overcrowded corner of Manhattan. Never have the
Jewish Syrians in New York lived very far from their Christian
compatriots, who initially settled farther downtown along Rector
Street, in a neighborhood near the future site of the World Trade
Center that came to be known as Little Syria. Years later, in the
mid-twentieth century, those same Jewish and Christian Syrian
communities would both gradually relocate to Brooklyn (the Jews
along Ocean Parkway from Midwood to Gravesend and Sheeps-
head Bay, and the Christians along Atlantic Avenue in Brooklyn
Heights and Fifth Avenue in Bay Ridge), creating enclaves, bol-
stered by subsequent waves of migration, that still thrive today.

The rest of the Americas were also a popular destination, mostly
because those relatively new countries were becoming new centers of
trade and commerce. Meanwhile, the Ottoman Empire continued
to weaken, and in 1909, the revolution of the Young Turks toppled
Sultan Abdul Hamid II and instituted numerous liberal reforms.
Among those reforms was an end to the non-Muslim exemption
for military service in favor of universal, obligatory conscription
into the Ottoman army. Families were shattered. A massive migra-
tion ensued. Thousands more Jews and Christians left the Levant,
heading largely for the American continent.

Selim Salama left as part of this wave, sometime around
1911. The particulars of his decision to migrate are unknown.

The story has become distorted over the years like a game of telephone. The most widely accepted version of the story is that when an Ottoman military man showed up to conscript him into the army and called him an antisemitic slur, Selim Salama punched the officer and fled, fearing for his life. In any case, he most likely left without much time to consider where he was going. To board a ship bound for America in those days was to hope for the best. Very often, Ottoman migrants aiming for New York instead ended up landing in ports such as Caracas (Venezuela), Veracruz (Mexico), or Santos (Brazil). It is known that in Beirut, Selim Salama boarded a ship bound for Marseilles, and then another bound for Buenos Aires. This is only known from the ship records because a much younger family friend traveled with him. The two men shared a first name, but in countenance they could not have been more opposite. Selim Cohen Hop was both less mature and less physically capable than the brawny and rather brutish Selim Salama, his friend and neighbor.

> *Having settled in Boca and Barracas*, the story continued, *a neighborhood home to a quickly growing enclave of Damascene Jews in Buenos Aires, the two Selims both tried their hand as day laborers. Mostly they worked as hamleros, one of many newly blended Arab-Spanish words that came about to describe the work of a traveling salesman who sold goods from house to house with a sack (hamle) he carried over his shoulder. This was a difficult pursuit, one which called for long hours on foot, carrying heavy loads and bargaining with customers. Not a year into their*

stay, Selim Salama sent a clever letter to Selim Cohen Hop's parents.

"Little Selim needs taking care of," Selim Salama wrote in his missive back to Syria. "Send his sister Faride."

Oceans away, Selim Salama still yearned for a girl with gentle eyes and wavy brown hair who had grown up next door to him in the Haret al-Yahud and whom he had meant to marry. Faride Cohen Hop traveled to Argentina on a steamship that also stopped, among other ports, in Marseilles, where she recalled seeing many girls her age shepherded off the boat. "Don't go with them," warned another passenger, who had made the journey before and heard of transient immigrant girls trafficked into brothels midway through the voyage. And so she stayed put, bound for the Americas, and not a year after the two Selims first landed in Buenos Aires, they became brothers-in-law. Selim Salama and Faride Cohen Hop were married in 1912. Across the world, a new family was in the making.

Buenos Aires

WITH NESTOR'S LANDLINE TELEPHONE IN MY HAND, I dialed the first number that Abuelo had scribbled in blue ink on a folded-up piece of paper and stuffed into my jacket pocket before I left. It belonged to Dr. Adolfo Yunis, one of my grandfather's closest friends from high school. "Habrá que ver . . ." Abuelo had said, and one of the first things I wanted to do was to keep my promise. The phone rang for several seconds and for a moment I thought I would have to make a visit to Balcarce Street, all the way in the center of the city, near the Casa Rosada, the ornate, pink presidential palace. Just then, a woman answered.

"Hello?"

"Hello, is this the home of Doctor Adolfo Yunis?"

The woman hesitated. Then: "Yes, it is."

"Oh, good!" I said. "My name is Jordan Salama. I'm the grandson of his old friend Moisés"—I paused—"El Negro Salama . . ."

I heard a long sigh on other end of the line, followed by short breaths that sounded like hiccups. Only then did I realize that she had begun to cry. "Doctor Yunis was my husband," the woman said, through choked sobs, "and he died a few years ago. I'm very sorry. It still pains me to talk about him."

"Oh, I . . . I'm so sorry." My heart sank. Dr. Yunis's wife assured me that her husband was in heaven, looking down from the sky, probably wondering why after so many years someone who knew El Negro Salama had come looking for him. After a few moments of further polite conversation strewn with uncomfortable silences, we hung up.

I remembered watching Abuelo test these same waters for years. Before the days of Facebook and WhatsApp, the landline phone call always seemed to be his least favorite game of chance. If the person he was trying to reach—a high school classmate, a childhood friend, a fellow physician-in-training—answered the phone, he breathed a sigh of relief. If they did not pick up, or if someone else answered with bad news, he tried to brush it off, but I could see the sadness from the dazed look in his eyes. Even if he hadn't spoken with the person in years, even decades, their death must have felt as emptying as that of a close companion. He'd left his friends behind in Argentina for a new life in the United States, but now they were leaving him behind, one after the next, upon each of his returns. Transience, I was beginning to learn, also comes with its costs.

Later, I told Abuela what had happened, too afraid to break the news to my grandfather directly. Meanwhile, I crossed Dr. Yunis's name off my list. I'd figured that time might be running out to find the answers I was looking for, and this was the first sign that I might be correct.

———

The following afternoon, I walked a few blocks from Nestor's house in Caballito to visit a historian and writer named María Cherro de Azar. Her name seemed to be cited in nearly every book about Syrian and other Arabic-speaking Jews in Argentina, if she hadn't written the book herself. A preeminent authority on the community—and one of the directors of CIDiCSeF, a Buenos Aires–based center for Sephardic history and culture—she had invited me to her apartment, having emphasized in our email correspondence that I must pay her a visit before I set off for Mendoza and the Andes.

María was in her mid-seventies when I met her, with thin brown hair that fell just to her shoulders. She had a precise, enchanting manner of speaking, especially when she was discussing matters of history. Her numerous books profiled important figures in the community; recorded the history of its synagogues, schools, and other institutions; documented the meanings of its most common surnames; and recorded the words and idioms that formed its unique Arabic-Spanish linguistic blend. Her mind was filled with anecdotes and facts gathered from a life lived in the heart of Buenos Aires's Syrian Jewish neighborhoods. I wanted badly to speak with her, if only because so many family members had suggested that Selim Salama's story was an anomaly, if not a complete falsehood. I wanted to know if he was part of a larger pattern, if one existed at all.

I wanted to be sure that I wasn't wasting my time.

"Oh, of course not!" María Cherro de Azar said when I asked her this last, very direct question in her living room. All along the wall of her small apartment ran a massive bookshelf, floor to ceiling, stuffed with old texts in a multitude of languages, watching over our exchange. María's husband, Roberto, a thin and agile man five years her senior, served us cups of sweet Turkish coffee in glasses cased in gold filigree, and a bowl of ka'ak rosquitas—small, round savory cookies sprinkled with sesame seeds, popular in Syria.

"The turcos began visiting homes and ranches where no one else would go, to sell to people," María said. Argentina's European immigration wave in the late nineteenth and early twentieth centuries coincided with a railroad-building boom, and suddenly the farthest frontiers of the countryside—long populated by Indigenous communities, who were in many areas violently displaced by this expansion—were within much easier reach of the capital. She explained that Ashkenazi Jewish immigrants to Argentina often established agricultural settlements, the most famous one called Moisés Ville, in the rural Pampas—initiatives largely backed by European tycoons like Baron Maurice de Hirsch who facilitated the emigration of thousands of Jews out of countries like Russia in the late nineteenth century. The Arabic-speaking turcos, on the other hand, went mostly independently to sell in the northwestern Andes. The fertile, hilly climate remarkably similar to that of the Levant meant that people from the hills of Syria and Lebanon, largely of Christian faith, were already settling there—and the fast-growing revenue from their vineyards and olive groves and apricot orchards meant that money could be spent on goods from elsewhere. Other turcos went to Patagonia, land of wool and minerals, or the Pampas, where the meat export industry was quickly leading to the privatization of property and livestock.

All across the vast Argentine countryside during the first

decades of the twentieth century, people began to increasingly rely on turco peddlers to supply them with modern conveniences, such as cotton clothing, for which they would often pay high premiums. "The turcos brought things that would improve people's quality of life," María told me, "because there was nothing available in the countryside in those days. Nothing! When the turco brought bread or flour, it was like a miracle. Hygiene products, cotton, medicines, too." She said that Syrian Jewish peddlers on the frontier kept close commercial and social ties to their compatriots in the capital, creating a thriving ethnoreligious micro-economy. The same trains that brought agricultural products to the smog-choked markets of Once and Abasto often returned with fabric and other commodities ready for sale in the interior, and facilitated the mobility and reach of the merchants, too.

My own great-grandfather, María surmised, likely moved to Mendoza at the urging of a relative or close friend who sent him merchandise on one of these trains from Buenos Aires as a business partner. With his young family somewhat settled in the provincial capital, Selim Salama began to sell. Perhaps he quickly realized that he could continue farther and farther north, where there was less competition, and began filling a horse-drawn cart to the brim with goods, mostly clothes. He slept in trading outposts along the road, and in the ranch houses and sheds of his clients. Soon Selim Salama was gone for monthslong stretches of the year.

The turcos exchanged more than just physical materials, María added. "In their travels on the train and on the road, the turcos learned things," she said, her eyes now wide with excitement. "They made friends. They learned how to play cards. They started drinking alcohol to stave off the cold. They sang, they danced tangos, they heard the folk music of the Andes for the first time. They became fluent in Spanish. They learned the Indigenous customs and legends of the north, like the Pachamama, the Mother Earth."

The small apartment was quiet but electric. An aura of great mystery had dawned upon the room. I got the tremendous sense that María wanted to be able to join me on this adventure that awaited. But never before had I been so sure that this journey was something that I would have to do on my own. Perhaps María knew this as well. "The turcos became Argentine in their travels," she told me as I stepped out onto the street. "Maybe you will, too."

Mendoza

MENDOZA WAS BLUSTERY AND FREEZING COLD when I arrived to begin my trek north. The sky was gray, and thick fog obscured Aconcagua, the tallest mountain in the Americas, and my first glimpse of the Andes. Mendoza is Argentina's third-largest city, a sprawling metropolis at the base of the mountains, and I was alone in it. With little idea of where I might go, I asked a taxi driver to take me to the only place in the city whose name I knew by heart: the stadium of the soccer team Godoy Cruz. The stadium was empty, but I asked someone to take my picture in front of it anyway.

After several hours of ambling around, wrapped up tight in a coat, scarf, and hat, I walked into a hostel that looked like a rustic wooden lodge, tucked away on a private garden property near the center of town. I uncovered my face in front of a roaring fireplace and felt my cheeks turn rosy in the warmth. I paid for a single bed in a room filled with empty bunks and went out again to find food. I came back with a steak-and-fried-egg sandwich—lomo a caballo, as it's known—soon after the sun went down and it was too cold to be outside at all.

I ate my sandwich in the lounge, a room of mahogany tables and hardwood floors, in front of a small television broadcasting a soccer game from the third division of the national Argentine league. The teams were Estudiantes de Buenos Aires and Corrientes, from a northern province of the same name near the border with Brazil. I was alone but for one other man, who was halfway through a bottle of Malbec, that world-famous wine from the nearby Mendoza vineyards. He was thin, sixty-one, with a weathered face and white hair. He wore a celeste-colored bandana neatly tucked into the collar of his white flannel button-down shirt.

"Do you mind if I change the channel?" the man asked.

I was mid-chew and taken by surprise, arrested by his quick Spanish, not unlike when I was brushing my teeth that very first morning in Buenos Aires and my aunt Corina asked me how I'd slept.

"Está bien, está bien," I said clumsily, in a very gringo-sounding accent. I was saying it was fine, that I didn't mind. But back in those days, late in the evenings, I often found that even the simplest words in Spanish wouldn't flow.

"You know what, I'll leave it," the man said, misinterpreting my foreignness for politeness about a game he thought I was thoroughly invested in. He paused for a moment. "Where are you from?"

"New York," I replied.

"Do you have a favorite team?" he asked.

"In Argentina?"

"Of course, in Argentina."

"Banfield."

"*Banfield?*"

The stranger's look of surprise was familiar to me. All my life, I'd had an unusually passionate relationship with

Argentine soccer. In the New York suburbs, we grew accustomed to watching the Selección, the national team, in relative solitude—celebrating goals at home with just a few family members, only to run outside afterward and remember that everyone else had been going about their days as normal. My childhood was marked, of course, by the emergence of Lionel Messi, who burst onto the international stage in 2005; one day around that year, when I was eight years old, my father went up to our roof, triumphantly dismantled the old TV antenna, and downstairs plugged in a big gray cable box loaded with Spanish-language channels so that we could watch the teenage prodigy play for FC Barcelona.

Even into the early 2010s, many of the most important Argentina games weren't broadcast on regular television stations. My parents would drive with us from town to town in search of places showing them, usually bars far too smoky for children. We searched online for the grainiest of illegal internet streams, during the very beginning of internet video. And every four years, when the long-awaited World Cup appeared on the basic networks, my parents allowed us to miss school on Argentina's match-day mornings, knowing full well that here, life did not pause for the tournament, as it did there.

This was, admittedly, uncharacteristic of us. "Never cancel plans to play soccer in order to watch someone else do it on TV," my father would often say. Yet Argentina always proved an exception. I hardly spoke Spanish during those early days, but moments, players, and chants became burned into my memory, especially from the early Messi era. For my brothers and me, deep, fanatical knowledge of Argentine soccer made up for a kind of imposter syndrome. In the eyes of most

Argentines in Argentina, my family had long been considered "Yankees"—but in the eyes of other Americans at home, we were thought of as Argentine, an identity that is abroad so often linked to this single sport.

There was also a one-hour Sunday night highlights show out of the country called *Fútbol de Primera*, which I watched almost religiously. The country's domestic league is perhaps the most passionate club sports tournament in the world. Visiting fans have long been banned from attending games to prevent clashes, goal celebrations often lead to stampedes in the stands, and police use fire hoses to cool down the crowds on the hottest summer days. I studied all the names of the players—this was the era of Fernando Belluschi, Gastón Fernández, Martín Palermo, and Walter Erviti. I even knew the names of the neighborhoods where each club was from, though I hadn't yet been to Avellaneda or Parque Patricios or Liniers myself. I loved how the cameras showed the fans singing, the fields blanketed in pre-match confetti, the colorful flares shot out from the stands. The roars that came with every goal. I wanted so desperately to be a part of it all.

But I could not settle on a team to cheer for. Abuelo was born mere blocks from La Bombonera, the stadium of Boca Juniors, one of the country's top two teams; Abuela spent her childhood listening on the radio to the games of their archrival, River Plate. Their nearly sixty-year marriage was a miracle, in that sense, and I could never choose between the two. In 2009, when I was twelve years old, I watched on *Fútbol de Primera* as Banfield, a midsize team from Lomas de Zamora, on the outskirts of the capital, won their first-ever league championship. And I decided that if anyone asked me from then on, I would say that I supported Banfield.

"Mirá vos . . ." the stranger in Mendoza said, shaking his head. "Would you believe that. You're from New York, and you're a Banfield fan."

"Yes, it's odd, I know," I replied, chuckling.

"I support Lanús," he countered, smiling warmly. Banfield's biggest rival, from a neighborhood over. We became fast friends. The man introduced himself as Alberto Balaguer, and he invited me to join him at his table. He asked what had brought me to Mendoza. I told him about Abuelo and the *Historia Antigua*, about María Cherro de Azar and the history of the turcos, about Selim Salama and the legend of his long-lost children of the Andes.

"They say that my great-grandfather was a merchant in these mountains, and traveled by horse-drawn cart from town to town, selling his goods to people in the countryside. I've come to Mendoza to follow his route north, to see what I can find . . ." By the time I was done, Alberto had finished his bottle of wine.

"Well, you wouldn't believe me if I told you," Alberto Balaguer said excitedly, a bit buzzed, "but I am a traveling salesman, too." I did not believe him. I began planning my exit disappointedly. "No, no, no, let me show you." He disappeared around the corner and quickly returned with a burlap sack. From it he pulled out his supply: dozens of colorful metal bombillas, the straws used to drink mate. Mate—an infusion first made by the Indigenous Guaraní people in the region that now comprises northern Argentina, Paraguay, and southern Brazil—is prepared by pouring hot water over loose-leaf yerba in a small cup or hollowed-out gourd. The bombilla is the key instrument: a fine-holed sieve at the bottom of the majestic-looking straw filters out the leaves and stems and delivers clean, warm tea to the sipper.

Mate tastes bitter, almost smoky—a taste rarely enjoyed the very first time. The age-old debate of whether to add sugar to the leaves rages on. But mate is far more than a drink: it is company, and it is community. The cup wanders from hand to hand in a group, refilled with hot water for each person's turn. Everyone shares the same bombilla. Changing its position and disrupting the placement of the leaves after the water has been poured is sacrilege. This teatime tradition is widely popular in the countries of the Southern Cone: Argentina, Paraguay, Uruguay, and parts of Chile, Brazil, and Bolivia. Walk the streets of any Argentine city or town and you will see people drinking mate. Mechanics sip it as they work under the hoods of cars; couples carry cups and thermoses with them so they can drink it as they walk; families share it at picnics in parks and plazas on sun-drenched afternoons. Steam rises up from the small gourd filled with loose leaves, the slender, angled metal bombilla firm like a stem as it is brought to the lips and gently sipped. When I was too young to know any better and saw Abuelo and Abuela sharing it with my father and his siblings, I thought they were smoking some kind of pipe.

As a teenager, I began to partake in the ritual myself. So did my younger siblings and cousins. I have very beautiful memories of mornings mateando with our family, mostly around the breakfast table. On trips to the beach, Abuelo would bring a bag just for his mate kit: a Tupperware of green yerba with a very small scooping spoon, a tall silver thermos, and a cup and bombilla. As the years went by, he increasingly had to pack multiple cups and bombillas, because there were so many of us grandchildren who wanted to drink. Now I think back, and I am sure that those days will have been some of the happiest of my grandparents' lives. Of ours, too.

Over the course of more than a century of global migrations, mate has traveled far. As many Levantine migrants to Argentina ended up returning to the Middle East—either for visits or for good—they brought yerba and bombillas back with them. The emblematic Argentine drink became popular in the most unexpected of places, and today Syria is by far the largest importer of Argentine yerba mate in the world. Of the 44,000 tons of yerba that Argentina exported in 2019, some 34,000 tons, nearly 80 percent, went to Syria. Another eight hundred tons went to Lebanon.

Much like coffee or black tea, mate has become woven into the cultural fabric of the Levant, too. A heartbreaking, rather dystopian video from the last decade shows Syrian soldiers drinking it during a break from battle in the now-ruined city of Aleppo. A gigantic stone statue of a kettle pouring hot water into a mate cup stands in the town of Yabroud, fifty miles from Damascus, where the parents of the Argentine former president Carlos Menem were born. During a recent video call, a Muslim Syrian acquaintance displaced by war from Damascus to Istanbul noticed excitedly that I, a Jewish American, was drinking mate in my house in New York. Without hesitating, he held up his own mate and bombilla on his end of the screen. "Look!" he exclaimed. "Chai métte!" Today in the United States, in fact, it's often easier to find yerba at Middle Eastern grocery stores than at Hispanic ones.

Alberto Balaguer had hundreds more bombillas in his room. His luggage was overflowing with them, each one a different color and individually wrapped in plastic. He carried his entire supply with him as he traveled, mostly in the lands known as the Cuyo, the famous wine-producing region of the provinces Mendoza, San Juan, and San Luis. He bought the bombillas in bulk directly from factories and wholesale dealers in Buenos Aires and sold them here, for cash, to shops and supermarkets, and sometimes to individuals and families.

"Mendoza is the nucleus of the Cuyo," Alberto explained, and for that reason he preferred to stay in this lodge, strikingly called the Alamo, as often as possible. He began his trading journeys, which could last for several weeks at a time, here in the city center. After a few days, he'd gradually move toward his clients in the outlying towns and then the more rural reaches of Mendoza, still returning to sleep in the lodge whenever feasible. By the end of the first week, he might find himself in another province entirely—like San Juan or San Luis—where he'd repeat the same pattern of starting in the capital city and moving outward into the countryside. He had other central lodging spots in each of the provincial capitals, he said, where rooms regularly awaited him.

It was difficult, Alberto told me, to spend so much of his life away from his family and his home in the San Justo neighborhood of Buenos Aires. But that was one of the legacies of the traveling salesman, he said: the sacrifices one makes for his descendants to lead a good and decent life, an educated life. "Precisely because they've missed me," he said, "my children will never forget me. They'll never forget where they came from, and they'll owe it to me to be good people for the rest of their lives."

Alberto Balaguer was so emotional, so passionate about defending his profession—which, today, is not only arduous but also increasingly rare—that he spoke too quickly for his own good, wandering from topic to topic like he roamed the vineyards of the Cuyo, pounding his fist on the wooden table and on his chest and wagging his finger at me.

I asked him if he would continue working in this way once his children no longer needed his support. "It seems exhausting," I admitted.

"Well," he said, "they don't need me anymore anyway, really, they're all adults and they're working themselves . . ."

He thought for a moment.

"But this is my life," he said, slowly now, "and when I stop traveling and selling, traveling and selling, that will be the day when I become an old man."

Sometime later, a European guest at the lodge approached us and asked, in shaky English, what Alberto was trying to sell me. She'd noticed the bombillas laid out on the table— noticed us waving our arms and discussing back and forth with great fervor and energy—and not understanding anything of what we'd been saying, she'd assumed that we were haggling.

Hola Abuelo,

I met a man today who walks the countryside
selling bombillas for mate. He's not quite your age,
but someday he will be. I say that because while
you do very different things, both of you feel the
same way about your work. You never stop moving
because it keeps you going.

It is freezing cold here, but I've gotten very lucky on
my first day. Let's hope the luck continues. I want
to get farther north, into some of the smaller cities
and towns where it's easier to ask questions. When
you're in a big city you can be surrounded by all the
people in the world and still not have a clue who to
ask for help.

I'll let you know what else I find. Also, the man
selling bombillas gave me one as a gift. It is gold-
colored and curved. Now all I need is a cup and a
thermos and I'll have my own set when I'm back
home.

Abrazos,
Jordan

San Juan

RUTA NACIONAL 40 IS THE LONGEST AND MOST famous road in Argentina. It stretches for more than three thousand miles, across the windy steppe of Patagonia, up along the edge of the Andes, past hidden glacial lakes and snowcapped peaks, through vineyards and green orchards and river valleys, and into the high desert, ending at the border with Bolivia. It feels, in some places, like one of the remotest roads in the world, a seemingly endless stretch of stunning landscapes and abundant wildlife. Along Ruta 40 in Patagonia, huemul deer, ostrich-like rheas, and guanacos—camelids native to southern South America—dart in and out of the sagebrush. Shepherds on horseback corralling hundreds of wooly sheep stir up little sandstorms, cloaking the horizon in haze and dust. In the north, the road winds through mountain towns at dizzying altitudes, past salt flats and copper-colored canyons.

One hundred miles of this famous road connect Mendoza with San Juan, a neighboring city to the north. It was lined with plastic waste and dead dogs. Cuyo, in the language of the Huarpe people indigenous to this region, means "desert country," and to the east, dry land stretched out toward the horizon in colored layers: the bare, reddish sand, the brown-green cacti, and then dense shrubs meeting the descending blue sky. Visible to the west, at last, were the towering peaks of the Andes, which in Mendoza had been obscured by thick clouds. Lower hills, speckled with farms, sat in front of the majestic snowcapped cordillera. I was flying by, but the landscape, huge and all-encompassing, stood still.

It was late morning when the bus pulled into San Juan, after just two hours along Ruta 40. I was not planning to stay the night there, but I had to wait until late in the evening for an overnight coach that would carry me deeper into the Andes. I was without a place to stash my things, and my body ached under the weight of my tall orange backpack, stuffed with all my belongings for the monthlong trip. Still, buoyed by my good fate after meeting Alberto Balaguer, I felt a sense of urgency and excitement to press on. I took a short detour to the grounds of yet another empty soccer stadium—this time of the team San Martín de San Juan—before I decided it might be a good idea to visit a library. I spent a few hours poring over newspaper articles from the 1920s on microfiche. The microfiche revealed nothing—no familiar names, no mention of traveling salesmen at all. I soon became distracted by a group of four college students at another table, working together on their math homework. I walked up to them and, apologizing for the interruption, asked where I might have a good lunch nearby. They told me a few places and then, sensing my accent from far away, asked me what I had seen of their city. I told them that I'd peeked through the fence at the dark-green bleachers of the stadium for San Martín de San Juan.

"Tremendo!" said one of them, a girl with jet-black hair and kind eyes, more or less my age. She showed me her backpack, emblazoned with the black-and-green crest of the club. "We're fans."

"You should go to a game," said the boy sitting beside her. He wore jeans and small earrings and smiled generously. "Let's see." He thought for a moment. "The new season starts August . . . twenty-seventh. Around then. Will you be here?"

That was six weeks away. "No," I said. I'd be leaving tonight.

"Are you coming back?"

To Argentina or to San Juan? I told him I didn't know. I added that I was on the trail of my family, that my great-grandfather would have passed through here about a hundred years ago, selling things from town to town.

"Around the corner is a center for salespeople like that," the girl with the kind eyes interjected. "Maybe they can help you."

Indeed, their instructions led me to a social services center called Asociación Viajantes Vendedores de la Argentina (Association for the Traveling Salesmen of Argentina). It was for the most part an empty office, similar in size, layout, and smell to a car rental agency. Nobody paid much attention to me, so I sat down in a chair, picked up a glossy brochure, and began listening to the conversations inside. Individual men came in one after the next—traveling salesmen, I presumed, who were passing through to ask questions about insurance and other member benefits. The man who attended to them was called Ricardo. After a while, during a period of quiet calm, I introduced myself and asked him what he did for work.

"I am a viajante," Ricardo explained. A traveling salesman

himself, he worked as an employee of a large food distribution company. "Viajantes are different from the old-fashioned peddlers that you're looking for." Peddlers, vendedores ambulantes, like Selim Salama and Alberto Balaguer, work for nobody but themselves, acquiring their own merchandise and pocketing the entire profit, Ricardo explained.

Even within the world of vendedores ambulantes, of those self-made itinerant peddlers, there were variations on how people referred to themselves. There were ambulantes, itinerantes, and comerciantes. In some regions, the merchants would announce their arrival in towns and villages with a whistle, or chifle, drawing attention to themselves and picking up another nickname in the process: mercachifles. Among the Arabic-speaking traders, they were hamleros. Sometimes all these words were considered to be simply synonymous with *turcos*.

Regardless of what they called themselves, during the years before electricity and other infrastructure became widespread throughout rural parts of the country, these traveling merchants acted not only as providers of physical goods but as important networks of information where communication did not regularly reach. "Human newspapers," Ricardo said. Merchants from Buenos Aires would quicken the arrival of news from the capital to the provincial cities, and those fanning out from the provincial centers would relay such information to the more isolated communities when at last they passed through, often quite delayed. "Like the way our planet receives light from a distant star."

I asked him, then, if he knew whether some of the traveling

salespeople of any kind still working today were also Middle Eastern, or Jewish, or both.

"Ah," Ricardo nodded. "The gitanos."

"What is that?" I asked. This was a new name to me. I did not know that this word was Spanish for "gypsies," the slur used to describe the Romani people, a traditionally itinerant ethnic group whose origins are in present-day India but who have for centuries lived throughout Europe and now have diaspora communities around the world. The Spanish word *gitano*, as with its English equivalent, comes from the false but widely popular seventeenth-century theory that the Romani people arrived in Europe from Egypt, not unlike the misnomer that befell the non-Turkish "turcos" in the Americas. A historically marginalized and persecuted community, enslaved for centuries during the Middle Ages in parts of Europe, the first Romani people in the Americas were brought against their will by Spanish colonizers in the first two centuries of conquest. Many others emigrated in large numbers to the continent during the fall of the Ottoman Empire around the turn of the twentieth century, also like the turcos, and again during the Holocaust, when as many as 1.5 million Romani people were systematically murdered by the Nazis—well over half of Europe's estimated Romani population at the time—in a genocide that occurred alongside the slaughter of more than six million Jews. Today across Latin America, more than one million Romani people still make a living traveling and trading in countries like Brazil, Argentina, Chile, and Colombia.

"Hmm." Ricardo thought for a moment, then turned toward his colleague, who worked with him in this regional office of the Association for the Traveling Salesmen of Argentina. "José," he said, "how do I explain to this kid what a gitano is?"

"A Jew!" the man called José replied without hesitation.

"Very well." Ricardo turned back to me and nodded in agreement. "A gitano is a Jew. They are the same thing, really. The religion doesn't matter—it's the lifestyle. Yes, a nomadic lifestyle."

So much of the rampant discrimination historically suffered by the Romani people has been tied to a societal perception that they do not belong. "The Roma tend to be seen as 'foreigners' wherever they live and have been feared, subjugated and frequently ordered to give up their language and ways by Gadje (non-Roma) authorities," writes Hazel Marsh, a scholar of Romani culture in the Americas. This kind of othering is ever-present in the history and discrimination of the Jewish people as well—such as the antisemitic stereotype of the Wandering Jew, the stateless soul, the lowly nomad loyal to no place and no one and cursed to a destiny of displacement. It began as a Christian supremacist legend in the Middle Ages: "a Jew who taunted Jesus on the way to his Crucifixion is cursed to roam the earth until the end of days," according to the Brandeis Center for Human Rights Under Law. Now it is just another way of saying that Jewish people don't belong anywhere, and are not to be trusted.

For this reason, I'm always careful about how I describe my family's multinational and multicultural past and present to others who might not understand. I am careful to emphasize that in the vast majority of cases, my ancestors did not leave their various homes by choice, but rather out of necessity (and that any choice to migrate would have been perfectly valid, too). That in every case, they missed the places and community ties they had left behind and, indeed, brought elements of their past lives with them as they moved on to the next.

At the same time, it cannot be forgotten that due to persecutions since time immemorial, Jews have had to be suitcase-ready people. That there comes a moment in which every Jewish family has a reckoning and thinks about backup plans, about the places we might reach for safety if things turn sour wherever we are. For my family, and many others in the United States, these conversations have become more frequent: After the 2017 Unite the Right rally in Charlottesville, in which neo-Nazis carrying torches raided the Virginia town chanting, "Jews will not replace us"; after the 2018 Pittsburgh synagogue massacre, in which eleven Jews were murdered at Shabbat services. With the taking of hostages at a synagogue in Texas in 2022 or the worsening antisemitic rhetoric spewed by popular athletes and musicians. For Argentine Jews, perhaps it was the 1992 bombing of the Israeli embassy in Buenos Aires, which killed twenty-nine people; or the 1994 bombing of AMIA, the largest Jewish community center in the country, which killed eighty-five people and injured hundreds more.

We make these plans because we are not blind to history. These are very real, very scary forces that have long caused Jewish people to disperse and build new communities and identities and families in the farthest corners of the world as refugees. Often those communities come to flourish and thrive again, though it takes some time. Bigots rush to associate Jewish wandering, forced or voluntary, with slipperiness and disloyalty. Yet quite the opposite is often the case: wandering allows for connections with more places than one; wandering means widespread roots; wandering builds empathy and understanding. Wandering is sticky, each encounter shaped and somehow marked by the one prior—and precisely because it invites such fusions, wandering can be very beautiful.

But in San Juan, Ricardo was not finished with me. "In that way, you're like a gitano, too," he said, gesturing at my oversize orange backpack. He did not seem fond of either gitanos or Jews. "Because you're traveling like this, without a place to stay, with very strange stories to tell." I smiled weakly, backing out the door as he spoke, and continued on my way.

———

What is in a name? The *Historia Antigua* asks this question on one of its typewritten pages. Abuelo often posed simple questions in his writings, yet so many of them could lead me on tremendous, sometimes yearslong quests for answers.

When it comes to Arabs, and Arab Jews, both given names and surnames matter very much, perhaps because each one has long provided vitally different pieces of information about a family and its lineage. Last names tend to reveal familial traits, such as vocational significance: Laham (butcher), Habbaz (baker), Falah (peasant), Helueni (sweets maker). Others have locational significance: Harari (from the highlands), Chami or Shami (from Damascus), Halabi (from Aleppo), Ashkenazi, Mizrahi, and so on. Even my own abuela's maiden name, Oss (or Qoss with the Q pronounced by certain Arabic accents), could have first been Qosh, suggesting the family's origins to have been somewhere near the ancient village of Alqosh, Nineveh, today in northwestern Iraq near the Syrian border, historically home to mostly Christians but also some Jews who made it to Aleppo many centuries ago. For Jews, there are names of religious or tribal importance: Cohen, Levi, Yahud. Further yet, surnames can also attach reputations to entire families: Salama (peace), Moafaq or Mubarak (good), Hib (love).

"Let me put it to you this way," a stranger named Maurice Salama told me one afternoon on the telephone. He was a Jew born in Syria, now living in Brooklyn. Everything, Maurice Salama suggested, had to do with marriage. "If you're asking for someone's hand, the first thing their family's doing is looking at your name. Where do you come from? What did your ancestors do back in Syria? Are you from a respected family?" Maurice Salama was constantly analyzing people's names. That's how he found my father, from a list of attendees at a medical conference; all Salamas try to find each other, I've since learned. I myself have invited Bolivian, Venezuelan, and Egyptian strangers named Salama over to my childhood home for coffee in order to scrounge up any possibility of shared roots, much to the bewilderment of my parents.

In the *Historia Antigua* there was a second surname that constantly accompanied Salama, but which did not have as clear of a meaning: Huedaie, or ibn Huedaie.

"My father used to say that we were Salama ibn Huedaie, and that distinguishes us from all the other branches of Salama that exist in the world," Abuelo told me when I asked him what it meant.

As I broadened my search online in the months leading

up to my journey, whenever another Jewish Salama would appear—on social media or elsewhere—often they would present themselves as Salama Huedaie, too. Sometimes we would be able to trace our family trees far enough back until they met, a paper-trail 23andMe.

Yet nobody seemed to agree upon what it meant. Huedaie did not seem to indicate a profession or a location. There were some wobbly theories. The Salama Huedaie family from Brooklyn said it came from the Arabic root for "gift," another honorific. Abuelo had written in his journals that he believed it to mean "son of Jews," used to distinguish the Jewish Salamas from Muslim or Christian Salama families in Ottoman Damascus. Perhaps this was most likely: a Jewish musician born in Syria—who left Aleppo for Buenos Aires rather late, in 1986—suggested via email that Huedaie was a diminutive version of *Yahud* or *Yahudy*, the Arabic word for Jews. It also sounds somewhat similar to *judío*, in Spanish.

There was also another theory, more of a legend, that I liked. After posting this question on several Syrian and Arab Jewish heritage Facebook groups, I began receiving messages from others who carried the surname Huedaie: from Toronto, from Mexico, from Tel Aviv. Several of them had heard that long ago, *kan ya makan*, a woman from the Salama family was giving birth in Damascus. The midwife (*daye* in Arabic) did not arrive in time, and so the husband delivered the newborn child. "He is the midwife!" his wife proclaimed with glee at the brit milah, the ritual Jewish circumcision ceremony seven days after the birth. In Arabic: "Huwe daye!" And the second surname stuck forever.

One Sunday morning, early on in my research, I called

Adam Brown, the head of a research initiative called the Avotaynu DNA Project. Avotaynu aims to use Y-chromosome STR testing to classify every non-Ashkenazi Jewish genetic lineage on Earth and trace them back to a single pool of common ancestors. When I spoke with him, Brown's team had identified more than six hundred distinct lineages, or haplogroups, so far. "At this point," he told me, "it's a pretty sure bet that the new people we're testing will fit into one of these already-defined lineages." One of them is the single haplogroup of Cohanim, Jewish priests. Other lineages, whose members span continents and socioeconomic classes and religions and identities, can be traced back, through a combination of genetic data and oral testimonies, to specific figures. A Jewish fisherman from the Azores whose whaling boat was shipwrecked off the coast of Hawaii, or a Spanish crypto-Jew who was forced to convert to Catholicism by the Inquisition and then sailed to the Caribbean with the earliest conquistadores of Latin America.

Adam Brown sent me a cheek-swab collection kit in the mail, and several weeks later called me back with the result. Of all the unique lineages his team had classified, and had worked to whittle down, Brown told me, "You didn't fit into a single one of them." They had to classify a new lineage entirely: #AB655. I gave him the names of some other Salama Huedaie men around the world, and he tested them, too—same result. "Oh, also," he added at the end of one of our calls about Maurice Salama Huedaie, the stranger from Brooklyn, "only five generations back, you're related."

I almost laughed—leave it to my family, I thought, to defy

even the most scientific, technical definitions of belonging. But it was something: #AB655. I wrote this down in my notebook.

————

**Posted to Facebook group למורשת יהודי סוריה ולבנון
(To the Heritage of Syrian and Lebanese Jews):**

> **Jordan Salama**
> Hi, my family is from Damascus, we live now in New York and Buenos Aires, Argentina. Our last name is Salama ibn Huedaie (הווידיה or هويداية).
> Can anyone tell me what *Huedaie* means? Where it comes from? Or if anyone else has this last name? Thanks very much.

40 Comments
(a selection, translated from Hebrew and Arabic):

> **Rachel Moshe**
> My family name was Salama, and my father always used to mention to us that it's Salama Huedaie, like you said.
> My grandfather was in Argentina with his brother, and before the First World War went back to Damascus to look for a bride. He met my grandmother Hesna, but the war started and he stayed in Damascus and couldn't return to Argentina. Later on, he immigrated to Israel. I'm living in Toronto, Canada.

Yaf Mug

Rachel Moshe, Oh my God!! I'm reading your comment from Mexico! My mom is also from Damascus, Salama Huedaie!! And also went to Argentina! It's a long story, but I have more info!

Mimø Fässih

It also might come from the Arabic word *Al Huda*, which means "gifted" or "the one that gifts something/someone." The ending of your family name is typical Syrian. There is also a female first name that is Huwayda. This is so interesting! Good luck in your journey.

Liza Ambar Salama

For all those who are interested... My father is from Damascus, Syria, and my family name in my childhood was Salama Huedaie.

My father explained exactly what it is... There was a woman in the family who had started labor at home, with the midwife yet to arrive... And one of the family members helped her give birth.

And when the guests arrived and asked who it was, someone who was at the birth said, "Huwe... Daye." In Arabic: "He gave birth to her."

The original name was Salama. And Huedaie is a continuation of it. In Arabic, *daye* is the person who helps the woman give birth.

Rachel Moshe

Hi, Jordan, I talked to my sister from Israel, she said that my father told her that the name comes from a story about a woman who was pregnant, and about to have the baby at home. There was no woman around to help her, and her husband did it, so that name in Arabic means "midwife." And from that time, people start to call them Salama and Huedaie. Sounds strange but this is what my sister told me.

———

If the exact meaning of the family name could never be known for certain, I thought, at least first names might tell a more revealing tale. But Selim Salama was known by so many different names that it is still hard to keep track of them all. *When he got off the boat in Buenos Aires, Selim was given the name Simón*, went the *Historia Antigua*. It was common for immigrants' given names to be Hispanicized upon their arrival in Argentina, whether by port officials or the migrants themselves. It was also the case that many officials who filled out entry documents by hand were not familiar with names from foreign lands and made errors in spelling and in sequence, leading to discrepancies within families and even for individuals themselves.

Indeed, Selim Salama was known differently to different people—each of his names fit into its own context. On some official Argentine documents, Selim's Spanish name was written as Simón, and on others it was Salomón. At the synagogue, his Hebrew name was Shlomo, and yet many of his closest friends in the Syrian Jewish neighborhoods of Buenos Aires knew him not as Selim or Salomón or Simón or Shlomo but as Abu Daoud—meaning, in Arabic, "father of David," following a very Arab custom of having a nickname that refers to one's firstborn son.

In the Syrian Jewish tradition, parents adhere to a specific order when naming their children: the firstborn son is named after the paternal grandfather; the firstborn daughter after the paternal grandmother; the second-born son after the maternal grandfather; the second-born daughter after the maternal grandmother. As a result, names are recycled for generations, often with small variations depending on the land where the child is born. In Argentina, Selim (son of David and Amule) and Faride (daughter of Jacobo and Sara) begat a David and an Amelia and a Jacobo and a Sara before naming the rest of their children more freely. So numerous were their sons and daughters, and so important was this practice, that Selim and Faride accidentally named their third-born son Jacobo, too, seemingly forgetting that they had already honored that ancestor. Nobody knows exactly what caused the confusion— the child was born in Mendoza, while Selim Salama was off selling somewhere in the Andes—but from that day on, Jacobo I (Jacobo Primero) went by his middle name, Alberto, and the younger Jacobo II (Jacobo Segundo) got to keep his first name (though, years later, in his young adulthood, even Jacobo II would go on to abandon his name for one that sounded less Jewish, and took on the more generic pseudonym

"Juan Vargas"). It is said in such families that when a name disappears, so too does a memory.

In the process of learning all this, I realized that my own name didn't fit the pattern. As the firstborn son, I should have been named Moisés—for Abuelo, my paternal grand-father. But my parents—perhaps somewhat overwhelmed by the many different traditions fused within the Jewish fam-ily of mixed Syrian Argentine and Iraqi descent that they had created in America—didn't know it was appropriate to name a child after a relative who was, thankfully, still alive. In Ashkenazi communities, which dominate in the United States, children are only named for ancestors who are already dead. So I was named Jordan David Salama, for no one in particular.

For a while it bothered me, this idea that I was the first break in a line of hundreds of years of tradition. I didn't want to change my everyday name, but I wondered if I should go to the courthouse to add Moisés, symbolically, as another middle name on my legal documents. This was, indeed, more common practice now among my father's generation, and mine—for whom more recent migrations and the passage of time meant that parents compromised and gave their chil-dren multiple names: one more modern and colloquial, and the other an inherited honorific, which was often more old-fashioned. At birth, my uncle was named Simon Victor, for Selim; my father Isaac Carlos, for Abuela's father; my aunt Florinda Daniella, for Selim's wife Faride.

My given name, instead of giving any indication of my an-cestry, only revealed to people that I was from the United

States. And in the United States, it is such a normal name that people say it quickly, without much thought, assimilating the consonants and shortening the vowels. Only in Argentina—a country where the name Jordan hardly existed at all, except on shoes and in the NBA—did my name give people pause. I was called *Shorthan*, an Argentinized version of the word. You could make out each of the syllables and the sounds when it was pronounced this way—*Shorthan*—so long and so drawn out. I liked that. It was a name that meant something, even if only to me.

PART II

Chilecito

THE OVERNIGHT BUS FROM SAN JUAN ARRIVED just before six in Chilecito, a picturesque old silver-mining town on the slopes of the Andes. The sun rose no earlier than 7:30 on most winter mornings, so the streets were empty. Only the light from the stars allowed me to make out the endless wall of jagged black silhouettes that loomed over the western edge of town. This was the base of the cordillera. My plan in Chilecito was to finally seek out some kind of community—of turcos, maybe even Jews—who might know enough to get me one step closer to the Lost Salamas.

The other passengers quickly vanished into the black shadows that surrounded the bright but unheated bus terminal. I got into the only taxi waiting outside.

"Take me to whatever's open, please," I said to the driver. "A café or something."

"You're alone?" He peered at me through the rearview mirror.

"No," I lied. I was traveling by myself, of course, but better for people to think that I wasn't completely on my own, I thought.

The cab driver didn't seem to believe me. He gave me a

careful glance. "Whomever you're meeting, just make sure you take care. There's no one on the streets at this hour."

I thanked him and he dropped me off at the only open café on the central plaza. Like most towns in Latin America, Chilecito was centered around a main square. The Plaza Caudillos Federales was green with grass and trees and park benches, surrounded by storefronts and a large church. The café, called Roberta, had furniture and floors made of dark wood. A waiter mopped the floor. The only other customer waved me over to his table.

His name was Mario Jorge Jobador. He was an old man, with a round face, a white mustache, and a cleft chin. He wore a navy-blue flatcap and sat well bundled in a thick sweater and a woolen jacket, inhaling one cigarette after the next beside the large NO SMOKING sign plastered on the espresso machine. He stubbed them in an ashtray flanked by a classic Argentine breakfast: two croissant-like medialunas and a cup of coffee.

"Who are you?" he asked. It is an odd question to be asked by a stranger—not "What is your name?" or "Where are you from?" or "Why are you here?" but "Who are you?"—and in that moment, I did not know what I should say. I could have easily told him that I was an American, of course, but here that didn't feel like enough. The story of my traveling-salesman ancestor had me coming to terms with the fact that so much of identity is fluid, that so many things I'd taken for granted in my own life were far more Arab or Jewish or Argentine in combination than they were any one thing in particular, let alone simply American.

I never know which boxes to check on the identity sections

of applications and forms. Sometimes there is a religion question, but for me being Jewish has always been less of a purely
religious identity than it has been woven into the nuanced expressions of my family's Middle Eastern and Latin American
culture. Especially in the United States, people don't often realize the extent of the diversity of the Jewish diaspora. There
are Iraqi Jews in India, nomadic "Mountain Jews" in Azerbai-
jan and the Caucasus, Black Jews in Ethiopia, Jews indigenous
to the Amazon rainforest who pray in makeshift synagogues
in the Peruvian jungle.

I could have told Jobador that I was Argentine, like him,
but still I wondered if I could fully own that label myself, since
it was often the case, living in the United States with lighter
skin, that my family was perceived to be Latin American only
in certain contexts, and not Latin American enough in others.
I'd also so far discovered that there were new words and new
ways of presenting myself in Argentina that people immediately understood, words that in the United States—as a Syrian Argentine Iraqi American Jew largely alone in a world of
difference—would have made no sense. Words like *turco*. But
to claim that identity still felt unprompted and quite strange.

So, in the absence of anything better to say, I just told him
my name. "I'm Jordan," I said, pronouncing it in Spanish the
way I liked: *Shorthan*. Then, I added, almost without thinking, "My great-grandfather passed through this town a century ago."

"Ah!" Jobador nodded and flicked at his cigarette. "And
you . . ."

"I've come to track him down."

"Why?"

"Well, I'm interested," I said. "He was a traveling salesman. He had a horse-drawn cart, and he sold fabrics and clothes."

"Turco?" Jobador smiled. He was born in Chilecito, had lived there all his life. He remembered the traders of his childhood who came through the town, which had become a major stopping point along the route north because of its once-important mines. "The men would arrive alone on horseback, and in tired caravans of mules and llamas, from the Miranda Pass and the town of Nonogasta, to the south," he said. "After a few days in Chilecito, the traders would continue on toward other settlements in the mountains, or through passes down to the valley towns below." A mine called La Mejicana, located at a high altitude amid the snowcapped peaks, gave Chilecito life in the eighteenth and nineteenth centuries through its extraction of gold, silver, and other valuable minerals, and led in turn to an influx of English and German immigrant miners whose possession of silver and willingness to spend was quickly picked up on by the business-minded turcos. Though the mine itself was long defunct, a few tangible traces remained of this history. One was a long-abandoned cable car system whose lines stretched up into the clouds. Another was the abundance of Middle Eastern merchant families sprinkled about the town.

I told him that I was looking precisely for them.

"Next door to this café, there is a shoe store," Jobador said. "It is run by turcos, descendants of those old trading families who came here one day and decided to stay. Ask for Justo Malek, 'Don Justo.' I'm sure he will have some helpful information for you." He paused to flick his cigarette, and then looked up at me again. "So that you can understand."

———

It felt right that my first encounter with a family of turcos in Argentina besides my own would take place in a clothing store. While the first generation of Arab Jewish immigrants to Argentina were mostly itinerants who sold textiles and other fabrics on the road, as the twentieth century wore on, their children largely began to sell them in brick-and-mortar stores. Now, entire districts of the Argentine capital are known for their turco-owned shops—marked by huge rolls of bulk fabrics in every color; boxes of socks, brassieres, and pantyhose; and suits and dresses hanging in the windows. "The eleventh commandment of the turcos is 'you shall buy and sell clothes.'" Back in Buenos Aires, my father's cousin Nestor laughed as he repeated a proud quip of Argentina's Arab Jews. He himself had taken over his late father's small shop decades ago, selling undergarments.

The Malek family's shoe store, on the central plaza, was small with walls crammed floor to ceiling with shoeboxes of all colors. Two large, brown, shaggy-haired dogs ran in and out of the open doors, which made the store feel more like a home. The family operation was managed by Don Justo and powered by his dozens of children and grandchildren and a constant supply of Turkish coffee. I asked for Don Justo himself, but a thick-bearded teenager at the register named Juampi informed me that his eighty-year-old grandfather was away on vacation and would not be back for another few days. He invited me to have a seat until another of his older relatives inevitably passed by, and he offered me a cup of coffee while I waited. Qahwah turkiyya—as it's known in Arabic—is black, strong, and unfiltered, heated in a copper pot my family always called a finjan, and sipped slowly from tiny cups. I took a swig and found myself coughing from the bitter, silty coffee grounds that rushed onto my tongue. Juampi and I both laughed at my mistake.

"Where are you from?" he asked. There wasn't exactly an abundance of customers around, so two of Juampi's cousins joined us, curious about what I was looking for in Chilecito. I told them I was from a Syrian family. It turned out that they, too, were Syrians—Syrian Christians. Juampi asked me my religion. I hesitated before answering that I was Jewish, but he smiled.

"We're cousins, hermano. From the same land."

He extended his hand. Relieved, I gave him a hug. How sad it was that I found his response so surprising. To tell a stranger that you are Jewish too often invites an unwanted comment, joke, or recoil. It is easy to forget that until the twentieth century, when nationalism and conflict began to tear Arabs and Jews apart, Jews lived in relative peace, and sometimes even prosperity, in Arab lands for hundreds of years. "Lifestyles, language, and culture created a common identity that centered on a sense of belonging to a place and to the people who lived there," writes the scholar Menachem Klein in his book *Lives in Common*. Jewish Iraqis, for instance, founded cultural institutions like movie theaters and newspapers; they studied at universities and ran businesses together with their Muslim and Christian neighbors; some even served in high-ranking government positions. In Palestinian cities like Hebron—before they were occupied and contested and became known to the world as perpetual flash points in the

Arab-Israeli conflict—Jews heard the muezzin's sunset call to worship from the minarets and the mosques and knew that it was time for their own evening prayers. The notion of an Arab Jewish identity went further than just coexistence: it was a shared culture, with overlapping language, customs, superstitions, music, and food.

A second cup of coffee nearly led to a third before Juampi's uncle appeared outside the store. Juampi bolted out the door, followed by one of the dogs, to bring him in. His name was Roberto Abilar, an older in-law whose family came from the largely Christian village of Aintoura, Lebanon. They'd been in Chilecito and its surroundings since 1914. His grandfather first came alone to scope out the region because he'd heard it had a very similar climate to that of the dry mountainous lands of the Levant. The men in his family had been peddlers who traveled much of the Andes to the north and south, just like Selim Salama—perhaps even *alongside* Selim Salama. It was a family trade that ended with Abilar's father.

"It was a deadly and dangerous road to travel in those days, desolate and unpopulated," Abilar said, nodding in the general direction of Ruta Nacional 40, now the longest highway in Argentina, traversed by our wandering ancestors when it was still made entirely of gravel and dirt. Initially, the older man seemed bewildered by my presence. He had been pulled unexpectedly into the store. He seemed out of place seated on a stool next to the cash register, his thinning hair freshly whipped and frizzed by the wind outside. But the store was warm and comfortable, and its light-brown décor was the same color as the land along the road.

He soon settled into a story, explaining how turcos were

prime targets for robbery and assault because they carried all their merchandise with them as they traveled. Well-connected merchants historically moved in larger caravans, he continued, usually with trusted Indigenous guides. Those who were less fortunate traveled in pairs or alone, often with as little as one horse or mule, and therefore were far more vulnerable.

Between 1904 and 1909, in the sparsely inhabited Patagonian province of Río Negro, at least sixty Middle Eastern merchants disappeared while out peddling their goods, never to be seen again (their families claimed the figure to be much higher, more than one hundred victims). Several Mapuche men, indigenous to southern Chile and Argentina, were arrested and were said to have not only killed but eaten the mercachifles in brutal depictions of cannibalism that were almost certainly inflated or contrived by pervasive anti-Indigenous racism within the government, police, and press at the time. By the turn of the twentieth century, so many Ottoman immigrants worked as mercachifles in the provinces that they also became scapegoats to justify a broad array of racist and unequal policies that encouraged the "orderly" agricultural and industrial settlement of the Argentine countryside, and in turn the continued conquest and suppression of the Indigenous peoples who lived there—an Argentine manifest destiny of sorts. Some Spanish-descended Argentine citizens claimed that the immigrants' informal peddling was directly harming their own economic interests as landowners and businesspeople. Stereotypes about the turcos were used as justification for the continued subjugation of purportedly "threatening" Indigenous people in the countryside—by wealthy landowners, for example, who accused turcos of arming their Indigenous workers with guns and ammunition.

Nevertheless, the prolonged event that became known as La matanza de los turcos, or the Slaughter of the Turks, sent waves of terror among turco peddlers across Argentina. In a world where each day was a gamble, steps were taken to combat these fears. One particularly wealthy Jewish trader from Chilecito, a man by the name of Abram Abravanel, was advised by police to carry a pistol on his lonely route north and would fire in the air repeatedly in order to scare off would-be bandits. I imagined Selim Salama alone like this, finding his way through this country that was not his own, in the hopes that it would someday be that of his descendants.

Roberto Abilar recounted these tales with an unsettling familiarity. He suggested that our ancestors had to have known these stories, too, and had the same fears, for the community of traveling turcos was very tight-knit, and everyone passed through Chilecito. He gave me the phone number of a friend—an amateur historian in town who had a book from 1917 that included a registry of peddlers like Abravanel—and wished me good luck as he stood up and returned to the street.

———

We're cousins, hermano. From the same land. For the same reason I hesitated to tell Juampi and others in the Andes that I was Jewish, it took me far too long to start a conversation with an old Iraqi man named Abu Zayd in New York. This is something I will regret for the rest of my life.

I was never sure where Abu Zayd lived, but I always knew where he could be found: at a small Middle Eastern restaurant in Yonkers, New York, that regulars called Ya Hala. At first he was its owner, and then he became its most loyal patron. He would always sit in the same corner booth laden with woven red cloth, taking his lunch or coffee or tea. I can still picture him there eating his favorite mix of chicken and labneh with cucumber salad, waving me over to join him.

In Ya Hala, the voices of singers Fairuz and Umm Kulthum rang about the dimly lit dining room, where dramatic Arabic calligraphy adorned the decorations on the walls and the doors. I used to think that it was the kind of old-fashioned café that could be easily found in Baghdad, Damascus, or Beirut, but instead it was tucked away, inconspicuously, on a busy road just outside New York City. It felt like the sort of place where people went to remember.

Indeed, the best part about sitting at Abu Zayd's table was hearing his stories of the past. Sometimes he was alone, but more often he was surrounded by other Arab men, each with his own tale of why he'd left home. There was the Assyrian Christian who no longer saw a life for himself in an increasingly sectarian Iraq; the old, displaced Palestinian; the young medical resident from war-torn Syria. The tastes and smells of Ya Hala drew them in, but it was Abu Zayd—a Muslim who left Baghdad midcentury—who welcomed them back.

Ya Hala was a place where my parents and grandparents, too, said they could truly taste the world of Damascene cafés and Iraqi souqs their family left behind. But for a long time, they worried that Abu Zayd and the other Ya Hala regulars would discover that we were Jewish and treat us differently.

Growing up, my brothers Jonathan and Michael and I often teased my mother for having what we thought was an irrational fear of being identified as a Jew. She painted over the Star of David on a duffel bag because when we were traveling, she didn't want people "to know." We were warned not to say Jewish things too loudly in public. Better to be safe.

These things did not make sense to us, three brothers extraordinarily lucky to have grown up in a suburban corner of the country where safety was hardly a worry at all, where any kind of violent crime—let alone violence against Jews—was until recent years so rare it was almost unfathomable. But my mother had her own reasons, and they were valid, for she grew up not in the United States but in Iraq—watching, through the wide and curious eyes of a six-year-old in the early 1970s, as two thousand years of peaceful Jewish life in Baghdad were crashing down around her. She grew up in a country to which her family long felt they intimately belonged, but which ultimately rejected them.

Those stories we heard as children—*kan ya makan*, of Jummah and Eliahou Rouben, of wedding parties held in luscious gardens, of flying kites in summertime on the cool roof—were always set up as the beginning of the end. Sprinkled throughout paradise were the warning signs, each worse than the next, until there was no choice but to leave. In the 1930s it was mostly political rhetoric; then, in June 1941, it was the Farhud, a Nazi-inspired pogrom that killed nearly two hundred Jews and injured hundreds more. By the 1950s, following the creation of the state of Israel, more than three-quarters of Iraq's Jews had fled the country; just over a decade later, around the time my mother was born, the 1967 Six-Day War erupted, and the few thousand Jews who remained saw their assets frozen and their passports revoked. My mother remembers when they imprisoned her father along with other Jews, remembers her mother going every day to the jail where he was being held, remembers the emptiness the family felt the morning after her cousins escaped over the border to the Shah's Iran. When she was nearly three years old, in January 1969, nine Jews were hanged in the main city square, accused of being Zionist spies. By 1972, my mother's family was among the last to leave, bound for the United States. Just three elderly Jews are known to remain in Iraq today.

Even some fifty years later, in New York—even as she forgot how to speak Arabic, her native language, and even as her memories of her birthplace faded to just a few fleeting apparitions—the childhood fear my mother associated with being Jewish never left her mind. It's true that, in the town where I grew up in a little red house with a yard on a dead-end street, it was apparent that people who were not Jewish thought differently of the families who were. They wondered, with good intentions, what we thought about the mayor's decision to rename the town Christmas tree a "holiday tree" (we had nothing to do with this, and couldn't care less, either way). There were also moments of clear antisemitism that, like mud tracks on a clean shirt, we would never forget. "You're not allowed to join Cub Scouts because you're a Jew." My youngest brother was just starting kindergarten when another five-year-old boy plainly told him this in the hallway. Another of us was in first grade when a teacher told all the children who didn't celebrate Christmas to stand up in the class so that the others could see. By middle and high school, the situations became even more overt—a picture frame defaced in a classroom with the word *Jew* scribbled across a photo of my friend; pennies jokingly thrown at boys named Levy and Kraftowitz in the cafeteria; swastikas found etched into the drying cement of a new school sidewalk.

As if being Jewish were not a complicated enough existence, being an Arab Jew feels even more complex. Along with the traumatic memories associated with being expelled from the Arab world for being Jewish, there also came widespread experiences of palpable prejudice and discrimination within the larger Jewish world for being Arab, too—especially as the Arab-Israeli violence has deepened divisions and made personal tensions more painful and pronounced. Among mostly European Jewish people in the newly created state of Israel, Arabic was seen as the language of the enemy. Scores of Jewish creatives who wrote prolifically in the language, many of them newly arrived refugees from Arab lands, felt pressure to abandon it in favor of Hebrew, English, or French—or to stop writing altogether. As geopolitical conditions deteriorated, this stigma extended into many aspects of life for Arab Jews around the world, in many cases pressuring them to shed their "Arabness" for a more uniform "Jewishness" that, of course, does not exist. "War . . . is the friend of binarisms," wrote scholar Ella Shohat in a landmark essay on Arab Jews, "leaving little place for complex identities." Historically discriminated against in the Ashkenazi Jewish world for being Arab, and with traumatic memories of expulsion from the Arab world for being Jewish, Arab Jews have, since the displacements, been made to feel that our multiple, interwoven identities are in conflict—that they must be kept carefully separate or can exist together only in private.

The very term *Arab Jews* (*judíos árabes* in Spanish)—as opposed to *Mizrahi (Eastern) Jews*, or the less-precise but widely used *Sephardic Jews*, to describe Jewish people native to the Middle East and North Africa—itself has become a charged and controversial one in certain communities. I much prefer it, not only because I like simple and direct language but also because I see it as the most accurate term to describe a culture that is an irreducible fusion. But many Jewish people who hail from Arab countries, especially those old enough to remember the displacements themselves, have come to passionately reject the label. "We are not Arabs!" they will proclaim, perhaps while frying kibbeh or listening to the songs of Farid al-Atrash, as if to say, We are not like Them.

And so at Ya Hala it was like an ironic challenge, to keep quiet about holidays and histories while we gorged on feasts of hummus and kebabs. But Abu Zayd, to his great credit, did not allow me to feel this way for very long.

"Come sit," he beckoned to me one quiet night a few years ago, when the restaurant was empty but for the two of us. We drank tea as Abu Zayd told me stories of the "old Iraq"— of street vendors who wheeled carts of sharbat fruit juices through the narrow city streets, of the fresh fish grilled over charcoal fires on the banks of the Tigris River. They were the same kinds of stories I'd heard as a child, from relatives similarly nostalgic for a peaceful Iraq that no longer exists: one of relative pluralism and coexistence—Muslims, Jews,

Christians, and others living side by side, no one group more Iraqi than the next.

"As a baby, I nursed from my Jewish neighbor when my own mother could not give milk," Abu Zayd told me, catching me by surprise. He'd known all along that we were Jewish, and what it meant. "Her children were my brothers and sisters, too."

I was born in the United States and have never been to Iraq or Syria, but I enjoyed Abu Zayd's stories so much that I started to go by myself to Ya Hala, just so I could spend time with him. "What are you eating? What will you eat?" he asked each time I sat down. Never, ever, would he let me pay. "How could I? You are like my son."

Abu Zayd translated familiar Arabic children's rhymes that my grandmother recited to me when I was a child, for his grandmother sang the same songs to him when he was a boy. We realized that ancestors of mine who owned some of the first cinemas and film studios in Baghdad brought to Iraq many of the movies that Abu Zayd most fondly remembered from his youth. I often greeted him with "Assalamu alaikum," and on Saturdays he'd wish me "Shabbat shalom."

For about a year, I sat at Abu Zayd's table almost every week. It was never planned—he was, it seemed, always there. But one day he wasn't, and after that he started showing up less frequently, and when he did come, it was clear that he was unwell, though he tried not to show it. He was losing weight and he looked pale. "Just a few things. I am okay," he said to me one afternoon, with a smile. "Thank God."

After that, we didn't see each other for a long time. Then,

one summer day when I stopped by Ya Hala for takeout, I found him back at his table, eating his kebab and labneh with salad, looking longingly out the window. I told him then that I'd begun to learn some Arabic, partly in homage to our conversations, and he promised that someday soon we would practice together at his table, inshallah. That was the last time I saw Abu Zayd. I learned of his death a few months later.

———

Hola Abuelo,

Why does a person only have to be one thing? So many of us are, at once, a little bit of everything, and all the while we are made to feel like we are nothing in particular.

Jordan

Andes

"FRANCISCO, TE PRESENTO UN SHAMI YAHUD." IN a fluid blend of Spanish and Arabic, Jorge Hanna introduced me to his son later that evening in their home, on the outskirts of Chilecito. *I present to you a Shami Jew*, he said. A Jew from Damascus.

"Welcome!" Francisco, twenty-five with a patchy black beard, gave me a kiss on the cheek but didn't shake my hand as he was wrist-deep in preparing a large bowl of raw ground beef. Jorge Hanna was Roberto Abilar's friend. I'd called him from the Malek family shoe store, and he invited me to have dinner with his family and some friends that evening.

Jorge seemed to know better than anyone the history of turcos in the area around Chilecito. He was a Christian Arab whose family migrated long ago from the Qalamoun Mountains, a region of Syria between the cities of Homs and Damascus now utterly devastated by the long-running civil war. Jorge told me of his visit to Syria in the years just before the conflict began, when tourists still traveled there in search of ancient ruins and narrow-alleyed souqs. "It was the most profound experience of my life," Jorge said. He knew no one still alive there, and yet he still found traces of home.

He showed me his home office, which remarkably resembled Abuelo's basement library—right down to the old Windows computer—albeit on a smaller scale. There, he kept a digital copy of the book Roberto Abilar told me about. It was called *La Siria Nueva* (The New Syria), a 1917 directory of then-active turcos—of all religions—doing business in Argentina. Selim Salama, deftly elusive, was absent from the list—he did not move to Mendoza and begin his trading until around 1920. But the book, put together by the Syrian-Lebanese Society of Argentina, did demonstrate the close ties among the Jewish, Christian, and Muslim immigrants from the Levant. "In the Andean provinces, and in Buenos Aires, there's a sense of solidarity among Ottoman immigrants from different religious backgrounds," Jorge said, clicking through the book's pages. "You know, unlike in other countries, where geopolitical issues and conflicts might cause problems." There existed, he suggested, an attitude of looking out for one another that grew out of an initial shared situation of uncertainty and new challenges. As something of an example of this, he opened YouTube and played the music of Azur Chami, a Syrian Jewish singer and oud player. Chami's name was an alternate spelling of Shami, indicating his city of origin.

"Chami became the voice of Arabic music in Argentina for all turcos, regardless of religion," Jorge said.

I found it fitting that we all huddled together later that night, Arab Christians and Arab Jews, shivering underneath our thick coats and scarves as we prepared a meal in the Hanna family's unheated kitchen. Jorge had said we would be having something called fataye, but I was too embarrassed to admit I did not know what fataye was. Only once we started stuffing the minced meat and spices into triangular dough patties did I realize it was just another name for sfeeha, or lah-majin, which I'd eaten at my grandparents' house for as long as I could remember. A popular dish in Syrian and Lebanese households, sfeeha are like Levantine empanadas. "We cook the meat at the same time as the dough in the oven," Francisco said, shoving in a batch of them on a large baking tray. I admired that Francisco, just a few years older than I was, knew these things—that he knew the meat had to be cooked at the same time as the dough, that he knew what *Shami Yahud* meant when his father said it aloud. I'd eaten Abuela's lah-majin for so long without thinking twice or asking where the dish came from. When I returned home a month or so later, I found the basement freezer, beside Abuelo's library and the *Historia Antigua*, stuffed with them.

The filling, raw beef mixed with fresh diced onions, toma-toes, and green peppers, oozed between Francisco's fingers. "All we need is mint," he told his father.

Moments later I was outside with Jorge at the edge of his property, sifting through the soft mountain soil for the stem of a mint plant. We were at the base of the mountains, a ten-minute drive from the Malek family shoe store. Seeing only what the narrow flashlight illuminated, I felt the full presence of the Andes for the first time. My nose tickled in the fresh, chilly air, and I heard the wind swirling through this valley of the cordillera. The mountains loomed over our heads. Looking up at the sky, I found it nearly impossible to distinguish individual constellations—all I saw were thou-sands, millions of stars.

The moon had risen above the dark hills: just a thin

crescent, still it was bright enough for me to make out that it was upside-down here, in the southern hemisphere, far from the northern sky that I knew all my life. I'd never thought to ask my grandparents if the moon in the United States had looked upside-down to them all these years. What small things would Selim Salama have noticed, I wondered, one hundred years ago, when he slowly traversed this harsh and silent landscape for the first time? This place seemed to have the power to turn even the most fearless person into a lost and lonely stranger in the desert, yearning for home.

With the sfeeha in the oven, we sat around the dinner table, tempted by the aroma that drifted through the room. Joined by Jorge's wife, Marta, as well as his friend Mario—who spoke in the harsh, nasally accented Spanish that was common in this province of La Rioja—we ate hummus and baba ghanoush as we waited. A major topic of conversation was something called the zonda, which was apparently fast approaching. Early tomorrow morning, I was told, the strong Andean wind was due to come down from the high sierra and blanket Chilecito in unseasonably warm air for the winter: weather forecasts were predicting a jump from tonight's 43 to a toasty 83 degrees Fahrenheit.

"Terrible!" Jorge shook his head.

"You're not looking forward to it?" I asked. Feeling rather depressed to have traded summer in New York for a July winter in Argentina, I was looking forward to the warmth that came with the gusts of change.

"Looking forward to it? Of course not!" Everyone else in the room scoffed at me as well. "We all get sick."

The zonda wind, as it turns out, also brings dust down

from the mountains and causes terrible allergies all across the foothills. Its effect is especially intense in La Rioja, where the cordillera is higher and steeper than in other parts of the Andes. While the zonda passes, everyone tries to stay inside, but many get headaches, and some remain ill for days afterward. The afternoon siesta—almost universally observed in this part of Argentina, where businesses closed each day after lunch and reopened again around sundown—would be extended during the days of the zonda, when hardly anyone wanted to wake up and go back to work in the evenings at all.

But that would be a worry for tomorrow, it was decided. Soon the sfeeha was ready and a piping-hot batch was placed in the center of the cold table. For the first time on my journey, I felt distinctly comfortable. I bit into one of the patties and the filling burned my mouth. I hardly minded, though, because it warmed my insides. I squeezed lemon juice onto it, trying to cool it down. The mix of lemon, meat, and spices marinating inside only made the dough taste better. A cloud of steam rose from the food, joining with the vapor from our frozen breaths in a windy swirl above the table, until I couldn't tell one from another.

———

The next day, the zonda arrived as forecasted. Also as predicted, I very quickly began to feel the symptoms of a cold. My throat was scratchy, my sinuses ached; that afternoon, after hiking alone up one of the tall hills to get a view of the town and the surrounding country, I tried to do as the locals did and sleep the siesta. But instead, I lay there restless, tossing and turning in my rented room, with a searing headache from the rapid pressure and weather changes brought on by the warm foehn wind of the Andes.

I turned the television channel to TyC Sports, and old soccer highlights blared in the background—they were showing goals from recent World Cups. There was Messi's goal during a 6-0 win against Serbia and Montenegro in 2006, his tournament debut; Maxi Rodríguez's overtime stunner against Mexico a few rounds later, when my father put my youngest brother on his shoulders and ran around our empty block with a flag draped down his back. In the 2010 qualifiers, Martín Palermo put Argentina through to South Africa with a desperate last-minute winner in a downpour that saw then-coach Diego Maradona belly slide across the soaking wet grass in celebration. At home, if I wanted to see Argentine announcers sobbing with each victory, to remember how we celebrated in the United States as though we were there in the stadium ourselves, I had to hunt for these videos; here such memories were so universal, so familiar that they served as white noise.

After a while I gave up on the afternoon nap and walked out into the winter heat, wandering about the empty streets of a mountain town still at rest. The only place open during the siesta happened to be Café Roberta, the same one that had been open before dawn the morning I arrived in Chilecito. At this hour, in this weather, not even the mustachioed Mario Jorge Jobador was there. I decided it was time for me to continue north. That night, the sunset painted the sand along Ruta 40 a warm, glowing pink.

New York

ON SOME OF THE DAYS THAT I'D SPEND IN THE basement with Abuelo and the *Historia Antigua*, I would hear shouting from the kitchen. "Jordan!" Abuela would call. "Come and *eat* already!" The food upstairs, it seemed, was always ready the moment we went down.

"What are you two doing down there anyway?" she asked me one day. "Isn't it all too much?"

I said, "Abuela, it's so interesting. There are so many stories."

To that she said the same thing Nestor had said when I got into his car my very first morning in Buenos Aires: "Es todo harta, querido." It's all made up.

One day, though, Abuela changed her tune. "You're so interested in Abuelo's writing, well, he's not the only one." Tucked away in a kitchen cabinet, beside the blenders and the Cuisinart and beneath a shelf filled with sweet quince jam, canned hearts of palm, jars of dulce de leche, and tahina sauce, Abuela kept a folder of recipes. All the dishes that she spent her life making, and we spent our lives enjoying—the traditional Syrian Shabbat meal of maude batata, a hearty meat-and-potato stew; fried kibbeh burghul; cheese-filled sambousek—were there, immortalized in their process of creation, another kind of oral history passed down through teaching and practice. But in the back of her recipe book, hidden away behind step-by-step formulas for the Middle Eastern dinners and the Argentine pizzas and the American cakes of which she is so proud, were what Abuela called her "poems." In reality, they were stories—one- or two-page pieces of fiction, handwritten in elegant, Porteño Spanish on neatly organized, lined paper.

Before I had time to process the fact that I had not one but two grandparents who kept secret binders filled with stories, Abuela began to read one aloud.

"I can read it," I told her, trying to pull it from her hands. But she insisted: always aloud.

"I want to make sure you understand every word," she said.

If Abuelo's *Historia Antigua*, and the extensive basement study of which it formed part, chronicled the grand, sweeping strokes of a family history as old as time—the movements and the migrations, the street fights and soccer games, the legends and the male braggadocio—Abuela's kitchen-folder stories, narrated almost always by a first-person female voice that she swore was not her own, were different. They ranged from love poems to horror stories. Some pieces had thriller-like twists and others were extraordinarily realistic, almost sounding familiar. At times, they also showed another side of our family's past: evocative, if fleeting, glimpses of the often-suppressed experiences of Arab Jewish women in Buenos Aires in what was by all accounts a male-dominated society.

In one of Abuela's stories, the narrator is sent to jail for killing a houseguest—a man whom she was told to call *primo*, cousin—who put his hand up her skirt at the dinner table, lingered outside her bedroom, and often entered the bathroom "accidentally" while she was showering. While she is locked away, she loses touch with her family members, who have migrated again and scattered about the world. In another tale, the trusted family doctor touches the young narrator inappropriately and kisses her on the mouth, her mother present in the room. Indeed, only in recent years—in an era of greater liberal expression and more female writers and narrators from these communities—have more true stories come to light about widespread abuse and assault in even the most traditional, observant Jewish immigrant neighborhoods of Buenos Aires: stories of women in Barracas and La Boca who banded together in collective protection, for example, against sailors from the nearby port who knew the turcas' husbands were away selling on the road for long stretches of time. There were stories of unfaithful husbands and scandalous affairs that were open secrets in the community, often contributing to feelings of humiliation and embarrassment among the women and narcissism and arrogance among the men.

Listening to Abuela's fictions—stories that chronicled some of the open secrets that were only talked about in private when groups of women would gather to confide in one another—I began to question my own motives. Was I promulgating these hurtful narratives by focusing on the egotistical gallivantings of a great-grandfather who could have very well been one of these problematic husbands? Why wasn't I more curious about Abuela's family, or about Faride Cohen Hop,

Selim Salama's wife? "I barely knew my mother," Abuelo told me many times. His living siblings agreed that she was often quietly overshadowed by her harsh and bombastic husband. According to Teresa, her oldest daughter, she was always pregnant. "She was loving, but she was not one to show it," Abuelo said.

The passage of time and ancient cultural expectations have occluded the stories of our matriarchs, but in Abuela's tales, I found the portrait of one fictional female narrator whose stories help shed light on those of many women who only now, in their older age, feel that they can speak more freely about their very real experiences and roles in a society that long valued them only for food, childbirth, and housework. Indeed, Abuela often wondered what her life would have been like had she not moved to the United States so young. Raising three infants alone in Brooklyn while her husband worked at the hospital, she filled what little spare time she had with books. A Colombian colleague of Abuelo's at work would lend her Spanish-language translations of authors like Dostoyevsky, Shakespeare, and Thomas Mann, which she devoured relentlessly. And little by little, she began to write, too.

As I began poking around our family's past, Abuela's collection grew very quickly. Every question I asked seemed to ignite the light of another memory to be scribbled down in the form of a fiction before it was lost. Some days, sitting at home, I would receive a phone call. "Do you have time for me to read you something I wrote?" Abuela would ask before proceeding to read a new composition aloud. Sometimes, on a particularly cold or rainy day when we were all at her house, Abuela would exclaim, "Let's each write a poem!" and all of us grandchildren would sit together at the kitchen table, often with mate in hand, and pull from a pile of neatly cut scraps of printer paper to write down whatever we were thinking about in the moment.

"Listen," Abuela would sometimes say when one of us would inevitably protest that the exercise was too difficult. "You are trying too hard! A poem does not have to rhyme. It doesn't even have to say anything important. Just write down something that is beautiful to you. Something . . ." She paused. "Something you want to remember."

"Oh, and one more thing," Abuela said to me in particular. "Write in Spanish. Spanish is such a beautiful language. A *romantic* language. Like Arabic. English"—she shook her head—"English is a language with no heart."

She knew that Spanish was, by far, my second language—that in Argentina I was constantly forced to answer questions about it from others. "A person's accent is carried in the sole of their shoe." An elderly woman told me this over coffee one afternoon back in Buenos Aires, after she responded to a post I'd made in a Facebook group of mostly older people who'd grown up in the Syrian Jewish neighborhood of Barracas. "It is refined by all the places you've been and comes to mark all the places you'll someday go." I had told her, as I did with many people in my travels across Argentina, about my conundrum with language: being part of a family that has wandered the world, picking up cultures and tongues and leaving others behind, I was surrounded all my life by relatives who spoke a mesmerizing mix of English, Spanish, Arabic, Hebrew, and French, but in my house growing up, my parents' only common language was English. That was what we spoke at home.

Often I would tease Abuela for this. "Why didn't you speak to me in Spanish?" I asked her, for the hundredth time, one Saturday afternoon at her house. "Oh, just imagine how I could be speaking now if I'd spoken it with you all my life!"

"Do you know how hard it is to feel like you don't have a home?" Abuela looked at me, serious now. "You don't because you didn't have to move from Argentina to Israel when you were seven years old, leaving everything you knew behind. And then you didn't have to return from Israel a few years later to a new Argentina, one that you hardly recognized. And your father, thank God, did not die when you were sixteen, ending your childhood right then and there. And you didn't get married at twenty-one, still just a girl, and only a few weeks after the wedding move to an entirely foreign country where you spoke not one word of the language there, either. Oh, and you didn't have to raise your three kids in that new place only to return to your country to see your childhood home, your whole childhood neighborhood gone and turned into clothing stores." Tears were welling up in her eyes now, and I didn't know what to say. "It is great if you want to learn Spanish. It is great if you want to learn Arabic. But you live here. You have a home here. You have people who love you here. And you speak the language here, and for that you should be grateful."

———

One day not long after that conversation with Abuela, she sent me a WhatsApp audio message. "I can see him turning the corner, his back hunched over," Abuela began in Spanish.

"As if he still felt the weight of the giant tray filled with Arabic pastries upon his head. He's looking down as he walks. His feet hurt. When he arrives at home, especially on Fridays, he empties his pockets of coins and hands them out to his youngest children. He showers, puts on his only suit, and walks satisfied to the knis, where he passes the happiest hours of his life."

It took me a moment to realize that Abuela was reading a story she had written about her father, a man called Isaac Oss, a baker and the most beloved baklawa salesman in all of Buenos Aires. This story, she freely admitted, was true.

Nearly every day of the week Abuela's father roamed the cobblestone streets from Flores to El Once, a corridor of neighborhoods long considered to be the beating heart of Jewish life in Argentina. These were loud and chaotic places, defined by storefronts selling a spectacularly colorful array of linens and textiles and yarn, by street vendors hawking scarves and newsboy caps, and by hushed groups of bearded men dressed in long, dark coats and black hats filing in and out of synagogues on street corners. Isaac Oss, a thin man not more than five and a half feet tall, weaved nimbly through the crowd, recognizable by the wide, circular tin balanced atop his head containing his creations—sticky squares of filo dough encasing sweet walnuts or pistachios, date-filled maamoul, and a trove of other cookies baked from homestyle Middle Eastern recipes he knew by heart. Maamoul is a holiday cookie in the Levant: Muslims eat it at the end of Ramadan, Christians before Lent and on Easter. Levantine Jews eat it on Purim, when it is filled with nuts, and on Rosh Hashanah, when it is filled with dates. It is possible that these other cookies, some of them

savory and others sweet, sprinkled with sesame seeds or pow-
dered sugar, were slightly more expensive—but the succulent
pieces of baklawa, for which he was famous, Isaac Oss sold for
just five cents apiece.

Isaac Oss grew up in the Jewish quarter of Aleppo, where
the days of his childhood were filled with ball games in the
dirt streets, and the clean, damp smell of mujadara rice with
lentils drifting through the lanes calling him back home for
dinner each night. At the coming of the First World War, the
struggling Ottoman Empire conscripted him and his father
to multiyear terms in the military, along with thousands of
other non-Muslim men and boys for the first time. Instead
of obeying the summons, the family fled. They boarded a
steamer and arrived in Buenos Aires when Isaac was just
fifteen. Not long after landing in Argentina, he met and
married a girl from Damascus called Bahia Frestahi. The
decision would present some challenges. Alepine and Damascene families did not intermix, but life in the New World
meant adapting.

Bahia was in love with Isaac. Besides his ability to bake
a baklawa more perfect than that of anyone else for miles
around, Isaac was known for a warm and affable spirit that
seemed to make the entire world fall in love with him. Isaac's
preferred spot was the busy corner of Larrea and Lavalle
Streets because that was where in the late afternoons school
buses let off the local Jewish children. Before scattering in the
streets and scurrying up the musty staircases of small apartment buildings to parents waiting with dinner, the schoolchil-
dren dutifully purchased five-cent sweets from the smiling
salesman on the corner. If they forgot their nickels or, more

often, couldn't afford to pay, Isaac the baker handed them their baklawa for free, for perhaps Isaac the father saw the sadness that came when his own children could not enjoy the same things as their classmates or neighbors.

Most nights Abuela waited for him in the doorway of their house. After spending the whole day on his feet, when he would round the corner of their street in Flores, he was bent over, exhausted, as though the round tray of treats were still propped on top of his head, weighing him down with an almost unbearable load. "Whenever I saw him like that," Abuela said, "I wanted to cry."

There was another reason why Isaac might have felt so tired after each long day's work. Years earlier, one day in May of 1948, when the air was crisp with the comings of winter and the whole neighborhood breathed in the first puffs of woodsmoke, Isaac and Bahia had announced to their children that they would be moving to a new country, where they believed they could envision a better life as a family. Not quite Syria but close, the parents thought, closer to home. Jews from around the world were moving there, they'd heard—mainly from Europe but also some from the Middle East—everyone hopeful for an end to centuries of holding their suitcases near, anticipating the next inevitable exodus.

They boarded a steamer, bound with high hopes for the newly created state of Israel. Upon their arrival, though, the situation was grim. Food rations provided by the government were not enough to support both a family and a baker in need of ingredients. There was a shortage of sugar for sweets. Their economic outlook in Israel was even worse than it was in Argentina, and for many Arabic-speaking Jews living among mostly Eastern Europeans, prejudices were palpable. It was very hard for Isaac to find work.

"My father first tried his hand in the port," Abuela said. "Then, he was a street sweeper in Haifa. But it was not enough."

The family suffered. Isaac and Bahia longed to return to Argentina, but they could not afford passage. As Isaac struggled to piece together a living, Bahia wrote letters to Eva Perón, then Argentina's first lady, asking her to help them return. Miraculously, one day a response arrived, containing tickets and instructions for their free passage back to Buenos Aires.

"Now we will go back," a triumphant Bahia declared, "and we will never leave again." The family split up for the three-month voyage on two separate cargo ships—a "world tour" in which the children delighted, taking in the emerald Mediterranean seas of Cyprus, Greece, Italy, and the French Riviera—before reuniting in Buenos Aires.

"We were repatriated in 1952," Abuela said. "But by then, my father was already beginning to feel ill. In 1954, he was diagnosed with lung cancer. They couldn't do anything for him because the cancer had already spread too close to his heart." Those final years were the ones Abuela best remembered of her father returning home, tired after a long day making and selling sweets in the city. In 1958, Isaac succumbed to his illness, and was buried in Argentina. In his absence, his sons became street peddlers, working in the city and the nearby provinces. His daughters left school to work in department stores and to help their mother at home. In time, from Bahia they would all learn to cook Syrian dishes like kibbeh and

sfeeha, ka'ak and maamoul and baklawa. They would continue to make these foods for as long as they lived, and no
matter where they were, they encountered memories of their
father, the smiling sweets salesman, baked into the dough.
"My father was a generous man, humble and unpretentious,"
Abuela's story concluded. "He was fifty-eight years old when
he died. I remember very little of him, but I do remember that
he died as he lived: without complaints, and without making
too much noise."

———

El Piano
(a story by Abuela)

*You know those things that stay with you from when you're very
young, coming back into your mind when you least expect it?*

*Those small, hurtful moments that become even more painful
as the years go on?*

*When we returned from Israel, my parents rented a large
house with four huge rooms. With a loan that a rich Jewish man
gave them, they bought all the furniture that the previous occu-
pants of the house had left behind. That family was also changing
countries. They were going back to Syria.*

*In one of the rooms, there was a beautiful grand piano. From
the very first day I saw that piano, it filled me with all the wonder
and joy in the world. Every day I went into that room and I ran
my fingers over the keys. I imagined myself taking classes, and I
constantly asked my mother for lessons. But her answer was always the same: the piano must be sold.*

I pleaded and I sobbed, but it did not matter. One day, when I came home from school, I went to the room with the piano, but the piano wasn't there. My mother had sold it to my best friend's family. I hated my mother for that decision. My resentment over that piano lasted for a long time . . . maybe even until now.

I do not know what would have happened if I'd had the opportunity to learn music. Maybe I would have been talented. Or maybe I would have become bored immediately and left it behind. But who is to say, if I was never given the chance to find out. Instead, all I knew was that whenever I went to my friend's house and heard her sister practicing on my piano, I felt a sense of anger so deep that it prevented me from understanding why she could, and why I could not.

Catamarca

MUÑA MUÑA'S SHOUTS SEEMED A DISTANT ECHO as I chased him through a maze of craftsmen, herbalists, and food vendors at the Fiesta del Poncho in Catamarca, a valley city of the Andes. Lost in the frenzied fair, my only guide was running away from me. I was desperate to keep track of the man. I stopped at stalls asking—out of breath and probably with an expression of pained terror on my face—if anyone knew where I could find Muña Muña. I was met with many astonished looks, and suddenly I was embarrassed again by the way I spoke Spanish. I was also beleaguered by a scratchy, hoarse throat and stuffy nose that I'd picked up in Chilecito with the coming of the zonda. But then two elderly women, who presided over a collection of ceramic pots and bowls, laughed in my face.

"Oh, you're much too young for that!" one of them said.

"And handsome!" added the other, winking.

I was thoroughly confused. When I finally caught up with Muña Muña and asked him why I was met with such responses, he called it "good business." And that was when I learned that the peddler Antonio Cruz was nicknamed for his bestselling product: *Minthostachys mollis*, known colloquially in Quechua and Spanish as *muña muña*, an Andean medicinal plant famously used, among other purposes, as an aphrodisiac. While I had been asking where I could find Muña Muña the traveling salesman, all those people thought I was desperately and unabashedly searching for muña muña, the herbal Viagra of the Andes.

"Muña muña para el maridoooo! No corte el tratamientoooo!" So this is why he walked around the Fiesta del Poncho so confidently, blowing a clownish blue whistle and shouting, "Muña muña for your husband! Don't stop the treatment!"

Those who did not require his services smiled and giggled when he came around. Men made jokes from a distance, pushing their friends toward him in order to poke fun at their sexual shortcomings, but they turned red in the face and quickly shook their heads when they were approached by the salesman himself. "Especially at public fairs like this, some people are ashamed to buy muña muña," he explained, smiling and shrugging his shoulders. Those who needed to make an actual purchase were more discreet about it, slinking up to him with their heads bowed. One man even tried to greet him as an old friend, with a few pesos folded up and concealed in his palm. But with these customers, Muña Muña seemed least discreet of all. He was a short and heavyset man, middle-aged, who wore a black Adidas tracksuit and carried all his product in a huge straw bag slung over his shoulder. He often tossed small clear-plastic bags of the herb into people's hands as he passed them by. "Good business," he said again, and laughed.

Muña Muña was famous in these parts. Torito Arce, a singer known regionally for his cuecas—songs in an Indigenous-influenced genre of music popular in northwestern

Argentina, northeastern Chile, and southern Bolivia—wrote a very popular one about the salesman. Videos online show Arce performing it with Muña Muña himself onstage, tossing those same clear little bags to people in the wildly cheering crowd.

At previous years' festivals, Muña Muña donned T-shirts and hoodies with his name and his famous slogan—"Don't Stop the Treatment!"—printed in large letters across the front and back. He also arranged fundraisers and clothing drives for children and others in need. As I chased him through the fair, he ignored most of my questions while calling out to his customers. I managed to glean that Muña Muña lived in a small town called Santa María, along Ruta 40, in the highlands of Catamarca. There, on the slopes of the cordillera, he collected his product: a bright-green, minty shrub that is native to the northern continental Andes (Venezuela, Colombia, Ecuador) but has long since been found growing over a wide range of altitudes from Venezuela to southern Bolivia and the Argentine northwest. *Minthostachys mollis* can be brewed as its own herbal infusion or mixed in with yerba mate. It is one of many medicinal plants used by Indigenous peoples, such as the Calchaquí tribe of the Diaguita people, for generations. These plants have since found use among relative newcomers to the cordillera as well. Enter any home in the northwest Andes of Argentina and you might find chachacoma, a shrub used for arterial hypertension; or arcayuyo, fetid goosefoot, for an upset stomach; or matico, an orange-flowered plant with antiseptic and anti-inflammatory properties for healing wounds. Since long before it became infamous as the root ingredient for cocaine, the coca leaf has been widely prevalent in Andean society, chewed or brewed to combat altitude sickness and a range of other ailments.

As gleefully as Muña Muña the man leaned into the persona that developed around him, the salesman's day-to-day life, as he described it, took a lot of work. He began his route in the eponymous capital city of Catamarca Province, a five-hour bus ride from his home. After a few days here he would move on—to Tucumán, or Salta, or Jujuy, usually following a circuit of valley festivals like that of the Poncho—and several times a year he would make it all the way to Buenos Aires, seven hundred miles to the southeast. His pattern, I realized, was not unlike that of Alberto Balaguer, the bombilla salesman: starting in cities and moving outward into the country, a taxing series of back-and-forths. But unlike Balaguer, Muña Muña had neither children nor much other family—he was a solitary man who spent many, many days of the year on the road. "Rain or shine, he just keeps moving," one stall keeper at the fair remarked to me as Muña Muña once again disappeared into a crowd. How did I ever think I would be able to keep up?

Muña Muña eventually led me past a small brick-and-mortar building with a sign that said RADIO VALLE VIEJO / 104.1. Suspecting I'd gotten all the information I was going to get from him, I gave up the chase. Besides, I'd happened upon the studio of one of the most widely heard radio stations in the region. From a tall tripod outside, a loudspeaker was playing the broadcast live to people passing by. One of the station's producers stood by the door. He could tell that I did not belong in Catamarca, but at first, he thought I was from Buenos Aires from the way that I spoke. I took this as a compliment.

"Tell me something," the producer asked. "Why are you looking for Muña Muña Cruz? Why are you so interested in what he does?"

By now the story I told, by nature of repeating and retelling it everywhere I went, was more familiar and more refined: I told the radio producer that I came not from Argentina but from the United States, and that I was looking for traces of my great-grandfather, a turco merchant who came west from the capital and traveled from town to town with his horse-drawn cart filled to the brim with material wares for sale. Rumors flew in Buenos Aires that we still had long-lost family in the farthest reaches of the Andes, and I had come looking for them.

"We can help you with that." Another man had emerged from the building while I was speaking. His name was Jorge Claramonte and he was one of the veteran hosts of that afternoon's radio program. He had sharp, angled eyebrows and wore a thick, dark-brown wool poncho. I followed him inside and waited a few minutes while he conferred with his colleagues in a room with soundboards and studio microphones behind panes of glass. Then I was ushered into the studio and told to take a seat around the table with Jorge Claramonte and his cohosts, and before I had the chance to think twice about what I'd gotten myself into, festive radio intro music filled the room. We were live on the air.

"We're back, here at the Fiesta del Poncho, and we have a surprise visitor," Jorge said in Spanish. "Who is it, Ale?"

"His name is Jordan—" said Alejandra Fernández, a co-host on the show.

"Jordan *Sa-la-ma*," clarified Jorge, almost singing my last name.

"—and he comes from the United States, from New York, with an experience that sounds fabulous, at least the way he's telling it. From the little we've heard so far, it seems straight out of a movie, really."

"Tell us, Jordan, what are you doing here?"

Kan ya makan, I wanted to say . . .

———

To: Moisés Salama
Subject: Radio interview
Attachment: Salama-Radio-Valle-Viejo.mp3

Hola Abuelo,

I'm staying tonight with a Jewish archaeologist named Daniel Delfino Edery. A professor from the U.S. put me in touch with him. He had a grandmother named Raquel Salama, but she came from Morocco, not Syria, around the same time as the two Selims. Daniel's son is ten years old and called Noam. Strange to come across a boy named Noam with a great-grandmother named Salama in a place like Catamarca, but I guess I shouldn't be surprised. There are traces of us everywhere I go.

Earlier today I recorded an interview with a radio station in Catamarca. I did the whole thing in Spanish, live on the air. On Facebook when they posted the interview afterward, they said I spoke "fluidly." And it's true . . . I felt like for the first time in a long time, maybe ever, the words flowed out of me like never before. Odd, because I'd gotten such little sleep the previous night, and because you could hear my obviously stuffy nose (I've had this bad allergy ever since I left Chilecito). I didn't sound like myself. My Argentine accent was so thick that it sounded like I was imitating someone on TV. It was another version of me. We bantered about soccer and I told them about drinking mate and cooking sfeeha and telling stories, as though I was an expert on it all, but really I'm just beginning to put the pieces together myself.

On the radio, I gave my email address and said people should contact me if they had any information regarding our family or the Lost Salamas. Someone heard our story and tells me she might have a lead: her friend, a woman who lives in her small town called Campo Quijano, near Salta, had a grandfather whose origins are unknown. I'm going to get there as fast as I can.

Abrazos,
Jordan

Campo Quijano

THE NEWBORN BABY CRIED IN THE ARMS OF HIS mother, who waited patiently with her husband in the civil registry of the town of Campo Quijano. I watched as the mother tried to hush her son, the father quietly filling out paperwork beside her. Their faces betrayed none of the stresses that so often affect new mothers and fathers; their expressions conveyed none of the shame that such a wailing baby in a quiet office would bring his parents in the United States. Here in Campo Quijano neither the workers nor the other patrons at the civil registry seemed fazed by the disturbance.

Once a frontier town, Campo Quijano was situated near a pass into the highest, barely habitable lands of the Andes, where the air was thin and always cold. I'd come here to meet Gabriela Caqui, an employee of the civil registry, accompanied by Norma Elías, a friend of hers. Norma was a motherly figure in her mid-sixties whose family had taken me into their home. News of my search had been bouncing around Argentina's rugged northwest for a few days now, on the radio and in local newspapers, which people still listened to and read in old-fashioned cafés with wooden tables and waiters in thin ties who served coffee in clinking little cups. Norma remembered that in her hometown of Campo Quijano, where no one else might ever have thought to look, there was someone who could have an answer for me: a woman in town who believed she had turco roots on her father's side, of unknown origin.

That morning there was hardly anyone on the cold, deserted streets of the town, save for a few women milling around a bakery that sold flaky medialunas and other warm pastries filled with dulce de leche and dulce de membrillo (quince jam). Wildflowers and dirt caked the cracks in an uneven sidewalk. Near the end of the main street there was an old locomotive, painted red and black and stranded on a stretch of abandoned track riddled with weeds. Norma and I stepped into the municipal building after a long and blustery walk from her house, my nose still red, runny, and congested.

Gabriela Caqui attended to us immediately, making space for our chairs and offering me a tissue. She was surrounded by mounds of paperwork strewn across several desks. "I'm glad that you called," she said to Norma, her tone serious as they exchanged kisses on the cheek. Gabriela Caqui stood out in Campo Quijano. As I was pushing ever northward toward Bolivia, most people in the small towns were of Indigenous Quechua and Aymara descent, shorter and with darker complexions. Gabriela Caqui was tall and pale, with green eyes that turned gray in the summer. But contrary to what most people assumed, she, too, had largely native ancestry. Her "gringo features," she said with a sad smile, were central to a mystery that had troubled her family over the course of several generations.

"In 1922," Gabriela Caqui said, "my grandmother became

pregnant after she met a foreigner passing through Cachi, a smaller village several hours farther up the cordillera."

Gabriela Caqui's father, named Claudio Cruz Caqui, was born nine months later. Her grandmother, ashamed, swore that the identity of the foreigner would never be known. Gabriela Caqui spent much of her life pondering the origins of this mystery grandfather whose physical features she so clearly inherited, for he was the only disruption in a family that had been in the Andes for as many generations as they could remember. She knew that Cachi, a major trading town along Ruta 40, higher up in the hills, saw many foreign visitors in the early twentieth century. She also knew that metal miners and migrant fieldworkers once used the road to move from town to town with the seasons looking for work, and peddlers used it to access communities up and down the cordillera for business. If any foreigner was to find his way into a mountain town like Cachi in the early 1900s, Ruta 40 would be how.

In fact, she went on to say, her own father had worked for many years as one of these peddlers. He possessed a disposition for movement that Gabriela believed he inherited from his anonymous father before him (along with, of course, green eyes that turned gray in the summer). Claudio Cruz Caqui traversed the foothills of the Andes between Cachi and Salta, the provincial capital, on the road that snaked out of the mountains through the Paso del Toro and into Campo Quijano and beyond. He led a pack of mules and cargo horses that transported everything from fabrics and clothes to cured meats and colorful sweets. Eventually, he settled here, in Campo Quijano, where Gabriela was born. Gabriela had never been to

Cachi herself, even though it was just three hours away from the town where she had lived all her life.

As she spoke, my head pounded. I wasn't sure if this was because I was still feeling cloudy from the ups and downs of the altitude, because of the allergies brought on by the winds of change back in Chilecito, or because what she was saying sounded all too familiar to me. My Spanish stumbled and slurred, and my foreign accent reemerged.

But I knew what I had to say. I opened to a page in my notebook, where on the bus out of Catamarca, I had started writing the story that I'd now told so many people on my trek north. I wanted to imitate the beginning of the *Historia Antigua* because I wanted what I was writing to fit seamlessly into it.

If this was her story, I said, "Let me tell you mine."

I told Gabriela Caqui that the *Historia Antigua* had set me upon a quest to trace my family's legacy of migration. I told her about the peddlers and the historians, the families and the strangers I'd met on my journey, and I explained to her that I was beginning to think about it all in terms of being rooted, perhaps in a place or in a kind of lifestyle, but mostly in the idea of a lineage, and the stories that come with it.

Still, I had not found a trace of the Lost Salamas, those other descendants of a great-grandfather that nobody seemed to understand. Gabriela Caqui nodded along quietly as I spoke, her eyes welling up with tears. If her father was born in 1922, I reasoned, the timing made sense.

"I'm here now," I said, "because I've been looking for someone like you, all this time, and Norma told me that you might be looking for someone like me." I thought it was very possible that we could be related, but I didn't know what else could or should be done about it.

For several moments, we sat in silence. The baby's inconsolable cries still pierced the air. Unsure of what else to say, I impulsively pulled out a family tree from a folder in my bag and showed it to her, to see if any names sounded familiar. They shouldn't have, of course, and they didn't, for the information she had gathered did not go as far as naming names.

Then Gabriela Caqui spoke. "It was 1912," she said quietly, looking at the floor.

"I'm sorry?"

"My grandmother in Cachi. She gave birth to my father in the year 1912. Not 1922."

Nineteen twelve. I had misunderstood. There, with a pang of shame, I could feel the blood rushing to my head in embarrassment: my Spanish, for all I felt I had progressed, would always be capable of failing me. Worse, this small but crucial error made all the difference. In 1912, Selim Salama had barely gotten off the boat from Syria, and was still navigating Buenos Aires. It would be nearly a decade before he brought his family to Mendoza to try his luck in the highlands.

Then, apparently trying to make sense of the situation, Gabriela, a Catholic like most everyone else in Campo Quijano, added one more rather strange thought—or at least it sounded strange to me back then, not knowing about myself what I know now.

"Maybe the Jewish people have it in them to move from place to place," she said. "Because of their history." Always building community in search of safety, opportunity, and freedom. Perhaps, she continued, her father might have inherited that quality, too, if her mystery grandfather did indeed have Jewish ancestry. But even if such an itinerant destiny had been passed down to Gabriela Caqui's father, it never reached her. She was still here, in this town where she was born and had hardly ever left.

It was all for nothing anyway: the timing was impossible. Selim Salama was not her long-lost grandfather. My heart pounded with disappointment and a wave of panic rushed up from my chest and caused my head to heat up, to get dizzy. I had come so far, and for what? There had never been anything truly missing, no insights that had to be found, no discoveries that my family needed me to bring back. Suddenly I felt profoundly lost and alone. It was not Selim Salama but I who had made the places Chilecito, Catamarca, and Campo Quijano relevant to my grandparents, cousins, aunts, uncles, parents, and brothers for the first time. In fact, I was the only one who had definitively passed through these places at all.

And soon I would again be leaving, moving on to the next town along the spine of the Americas, while Gabriela Caqui would be staying here, in Campo Quijano.

———

Historia Antigua

The Tale of a Thousand Warplanes

My father would spend weekday mornings sitting out on the corner of Calles Brandsen and Patricios, reading the newspaper. It was just down the street from Or Torah, the knis (synagogue), which was inaugurated in 1930 and was the beating heart of a neighborhood community of highly observant Jewish families from Damascus with last names like Hanin, Hasbani, Medina, Alfie, and Mouallem, who settled in these adjacent neighborhoods of Barracas and La Boca throughout the early twentieth century, slowly building an enclave in exile. Each morning on the corner of Brandsen and Patricios, outside the Muhafra family store, the men from these families gathered after early morning prayers at Or Torah to prepare for the day's work.

"One thousand Allied warplanes have bombed Berlin!" Selim read aloud from the paper one morning during the Second World War. I was there that day, watching.

The other men sitting around him stopped what they were doing. "What did you say?" Even old Muhafra emerged from his corner store.

"One thousand Allied planes, says it right here." Selim smacked the paper with the back of his hand. "If you ask me, the tide's turning. Soon, the war will be over." He was one of only a few in the group who read Spanish well enough to understand what was written in the paper, so most mornings he read the news aloud at this gathering over mate and coffee and backgammon. The attention was on him, and he loved this position so much that he did not always stop once he got past the day's news; instead, knowing that most of the other men couldn't tell the difference either way, he sometimes continued "reading" stories that were completely made up, acting as though they came straight from the headlines. They were harmless exaggerations, so much so that one might have wondered why he bothered with them at all. But there are no doubts about the pleasure he took from being heard. No one ever challenged him. He was, after all, one of the most

fearsome street fighters there were in Damascus, back when they were all still growing up as boys and fought teref u sef, sparring with wooden swords and shields.

But this morning, on the corner of Brandsen and Patricios outside the Muhafra store, a wave of murmurs and hushed whispers washed over the group as Selim Salama went on to describe the attack of a thousand warplanes, oceans away. The other men were captivated. Among them, however, was a newcomer who had noticed that same story in the paper just a little while earlier.

"Abu Daoud," said the newcomer, looking over his shoulder, "the newspaper says one hundred planes, not one thousand."

Then the corner was silent. Selim Salama simply looked at the young man in breathless silence, a piercing stare. Then, after several seconds, in a slow and unwavering tone strong enough to intimidate even the bravest of onlookers, he said, "If I said there were one thousand planes, there were one thousand planes."

And that was that.

PART III

Cafayate

CAFAYATE SITS AT THE START OF THE QUEBRADA
de las Conchas, a canyon that winds its way down from Ruta
40 toward the city of Salta. A river runs through the Quebrada. Now, so does a road. With its staggering cliffs, expan-
sive valleys, and barren mountains colored a hundred shades
of copper, it is the kind of landscape that makes you feel very
small—especially in the dry winter, when the river is a mere
trickle and land stretches across the valley.

"Surely your great-grandfather would have seen this and
been amazed." Nearly everyone I met in Cafayate said this to
me. Yet I was starting to become less sure. I was beginning
to come to terms with the fact that it would be nearly impossible to track down any concrete traces of Selim Salama.
I scoured archives and microfiches, newspaper clippings and
old books, and he appeared in none of them. He was not one
of the wealthy businessmen of his time, so his name was not
remembered like the names Zeitune, or Abravanel, or Teubal.
Peddling was mostly unofficial work in those days—cash and
trade-based—so it could have been that he was never formally
registered (though some mercachifles historically carried me-
dallions or slips of paper that served as their license to operate

in any given region). Only a handful of pictures of him have survived. From the perspective of recorded history—in the Andes, at least—he hardly existed.

But in lore, things were different. In Buenos Aires, Selim Salama would gather regularly with extended family and friends in the front living room facing Brandsen Street; in the afternoons, the next-door neighbors, the "Del Piano" family, would open their large bay windows and rehearse their music, the melodies drifting in and out of the halls of the Salama house and over the Plaza Colombia, a large park across the street where children would pick figs from fenced-in fruit trees. To entertain his guests, Selim Salama would tell stories, and some of those stories lived on.

Once, around the time when Abuelo and his younger brother, Elías, were finishing medical school, they invited two non-Syrian classmates home for dinner. It was a night of indulgence in wine and conversation about politics and medicine dominated by the four physicians, while the rest of the Salama family—mostly homemakers, shopkeepers, and fabric salesmen—listened politely.

But near the end of the night, the discussion drifted toward the Salama parents' origins, as it often did when strangers were around. Selim Salama saw an opening and entered the conversation the only way he knew how. "Let me tell you gentlemen a story," he said proudly. "I have nearly died many times in my life, given all the places I have been, and all the things that I have seen. But none was scarier than once in Damascus, when I had no choice but to leap from the ninth floor of a burning building!"

"Selim," his wife, Faride, whispered to him in Arabic so

that the two visitors could not understand, "inzel shwaye." She felt like she was always telling him "inzel shwaye," to take it down a notch. They both knew full well that there had been no nine-story buildings in Damascus.

"Actually, it was the fifth floor, by my memory . . ."

"Selim, inzel shwaye."

"Alright, it was the first floor, is that low enough for you all?" And by then everyone was roaring with laughter.

Perhaps, around the dinner table and on the corner of Brandsen and Patricios alike, he told these tales of fantasy, of heroism, and of great adventure because it was all that he could do to stay relevant in a new world—in a foreign, difficult world where he was no longer king of the streets but rather an immigrant outsider. Perhaps stories were his way of making sense of a world where he felt like he did not exactly belong. I figured as much because, in a different way, I was beginning to do the same.

Still, there remained the unanswered question of the Lost Salamas. Any long-lost descendants of his, if they even existed, would likely not have carried his last name, an oversight of mine that I only fully considered after I'd rather impulsively arrived in the Andes. This made everything much more difficult—that, plus the growing proof that my great-grandfather was just one of many, many others who worked in this manner and had such encounters.

Like in Chilecito, on the main plaza in Cafayate there was a store still owned and operated by one of the many Syrian families who came with the early trading days and stayed. Walter and Haydée Daruich's wine shop, Vinoteca La Escalera, was small but very well-known, crammed with bottles and wooden cases on display (Cafayate is famous for its wine, with acres of vineyards lining the road toward the Quebrada). In keeping with its name, much of the store was occupied by a large black staircase that led to what one saleswoman referred to as the "back office." I told her I was interested in speaking with the shop's owners, and it took several minutes of convincing and explaining before she told me to wait as she hurried up the staircase.

As it turned out, the "back office" was the Daruich family home, an apartment above the shop. Haydée and Walter, an older couple in their sixties, were having tea in the kitchen when I was led upstairs. The apartment was centered around one large room, a living space with an open kitchen. Toward the front of the apartment, the room was stuffed with boxes of additional products, piled high. A back hallway seemed to lead to the bedrooms and the bathrooms.

Haydée offered me some cookies and tea—with extra lemon and honey, she added, picking up on the fact that I'd caught a cold. The three of us sat down around the coffee table to chat. There are some people who have distinctly kind faces, I think, and the Daruiches fit that mold. Haydée looked strikingly like my great-grandmother Faride Cohen Hop did in pictures. Walter, her husband, looked very much like Mario Jorge Jobador, the older café customer I met at dawn in Chilecito a week or so earlier. He had a gray mustache, oval glasses, and a cleft chin.

I began by apologizing profusely for interrupting their teatime and barging into their home unannounced. They protested in the typical, exaggerated Argentine way: by throwing their arms up into the air and smiling and calling me "querido."

I told them of Selim Salama and his wanderings, and Walter replied that his uncles worked in almost exactly the same manner through the Quebrada de las Conchas, between Cafayate and Salta. I liked how in Argentina, whenever I told my story to somebody, they would respond with theirs, like a battle of oral histories.

Walter's grandfather Domingo Daruich, a Syrian Christian, was born in a town called Maharda, south of Aleppo. Domingo Daruich, like Selim Salama, came to Argentina around 1910 to escape conscription into the Ottoman military. Asthma and other health problems caused him to leave Buenos Aires with his cousin, bound for the fresh air of the northwest. He headed first for Salta, and later to the nearby town of Rosario de Lerma, where he operated a general store and started a family. After several years, his health worsened, and doctors advised him to relocate to a slightly higher altitude, where the climate was drier. The decision was made to move with his wife and six sons to Cafayate, where in proper turco fashion, he once again opened a general store.

For many years, the family business was not centered around wine, as it was now. Cafayate, like the lands of the Levant, was very conducive to the cultivation of fruits, olives, and spices, all of which were sold in the Daruich Family General Store. Selling everything from clothing to dried apricots, the store became a well-known provider in the valley both north and south of Cafayate. Domingo's sons eventually grew old enough to help with the family business, and peddled goods in horse-drawn carts from Cafayate along the Río las Conchas and the eponymous Quebrada that encompasses it. Because there was no reliable road through the Quebrada de las

Conchas in those days, to traverse the valley, horses and pack animals at times had to wade through the river.

"People asked for the things they needed, and the Daruiches delivered," Walter said, pointing out that their last name, more commonly spelled *Darwish* in English, means "wandering" or "roaming" in Arabic. "They were fighters, hard workers willing to do the difficult work to support their families." I thought of Alberto Balaguer, the bombilla salesman who, without fanfare, was probably doing the same as we were speaking.

Walter Daruich told me that a large number of turcos once worked the region, including a sizeable Jewish community based in Salta. But around 1970 came the paved road—now Ruta Nacional 68, which cuts a stunning, swerving path through the canyon and over bridges across the clear river—and this kind of peddling quickly became obsolete.

———

"Sometimes I wonder how you became a doctor when everyone else around you continued to work as salesmen," I told Abuelo one morning in the basement. I thought of young Juampi working behind the register at his grandfather's shoe store, or my cousin Martín helping Nestor sell undergarments during the holidays in Villa Ballester. My family's fate—indeed, the very reason why we now live in the United States, the very reason why my parents met and I even came to exist—is because Abuelo was the first in that long line of Salama generations to study at a university.

He flipped to a page in the *Historia Antigua* and had me read:

When I was a boy, in contrast to this age of technology in which we're now living, we were always moving. I remember that we had to walk to buy groceries or cleaning supplies. The stores were mostly on the same block where we lived, and everything was always fresh. But there were also people—like my father—who were hamleros, who went from house to house in my neighborhood, selling things for a little bit less than the stores. Some of them came in cars, like the fruit and vegetable salesmen, and others on foot, like the knife sharpeners, the mattress salesmen, and the tinsmiths. The milkmen came around in trucks, though on some streets, like Azara Street, every day we saw one with his cows and calves, milking them and filling people's jugs right there in the city.

It's not that I didn't do the same thing. For a long time, I did. When I was seven, eight years old, on holidays or other days when I didn't go to school, I went from house to house and sold combs, toothpaste, cans of quince jam. Sometimes, on the unpaved dirt roads, we would light fires to make fushar, what we called popcorn in Arabic, with kernels that we stole from the grocery stores.

We loved those roads—those so-called baldíos, wastelands. Ruiz Díaz Street, right by our house, was one of them. We made great use of it—our "barra de turcos," our little street gang, played football and had street fights there, and the little police cars couldn't enter because it was always too muddy.

But also on the same street there was a public library. It was called the Sociedad Luz (the Society of Light). Once I discovered it, that library became my second home during the last years of elementary school and all throughout high school. It was the cultural center that changed my life.

The Sociedad Luz had two floors. On the ground floor, there was a children's library and a number of rooms where they had *events and classes and other activities. There were courses on drawing and painting and writing. The children's librarian would help us pick out books to read. The first book that he gave me was* Heart *by Edmondo de Amicis. Then* Tartarin of Tarascon *by Alphonse Daudet, and then, of course,* The Gaucho Martín Fierro, *the epic gaucho poem of José Hernández. After reading* Martín Fierro, *I grew interested in poetry. I stopped fighting so much in the streets and started to actually enjoy school.*

In high school, I started going to the second floor, the "serious" library, where the older students got together to study. The librarian was called Zorzoli and he spent the whole day smoking. He coughed up so much phlegm that you could hear him from the street corner outside. We were not allowed to speak, and the room felt like a funeral. There, I read El Tesoro de la Juventud, *which was a kind of encyclopedia, and—pucha!—you have no idea how much I learned. I would sit there with the Masri brothers (Jaime and Julio) and Alberto Janin, the three other turcos who studied there every day. All of them became doctors. I followed their example and I decided to study medicine, too.*

It was also in the library of the Sociedad Luz where I developed my socialist consciousness; years later I became very active in the party and helped lead a group of revolution-minded medical students in the 1950s. From Buenos Aires, we took monthlong trips to Patagonia and the Andes by train, and we prepared, militarily, for an uprising that ultimately never arrived. All of that was years later. But in 1938, when I was ten years old, I met my political mentor for the first time. His name was Alfredo L. Palacios. He was a lawyer and socialist senator from our neighborhood. Long before I was born, he'd been elected the first socialist representative on the entire American continent. I remember the day that I met him at the library, because Palacios had given a presentation and I asked him a question. "Señor," I began, and he interrupted me.

"Jovenzuelo, young man, don't call me señor," *Palacios said. "Call me* compañero."

Campo Quijano

"COME IN, COME IN." NORMA SUSANA ELÍAS USHERED me back into her home in Campo Quijano at the foothills of the Andes after my brief sojourn in the copper canyons of Cafayate. It was dark and the wind howled with cold. My plan had been to stick to the high mountain towns along Ruta 40 as much as I could, but conditions changed quickly in the microclimates of the cordillera: just a few days and a few hundred kilometers after the zonda in Chilecito, a deep freeze had set in. It was so cold that it made the national news. Many of the passes were snowed in, and finding public transportation to get me up into the hills proved impossible. I hadn't planned to stop in Campo Quijano in the first place, but now I was back again, stranded, with nowhere else to stay.

Norma Susana Elías's house was not heated, but it was filled with warmth. The radio played quietly in the background while a large pot of locro boiled vigorously on the stove, sending clouds of hot steam careening into the air. For just about as long as humans have been living in the Andes, they have been eating locro. A Quechua stew of white corn, beans, squash, and pumpkin in a meat-based broth, it is nowadays typically eaten in the month of July, around Argentina's

Independence Day. Locro requires many hours to prepare—the longer it cooks, the better, so that the meat has time to become soft and tender on the bone and all the flavors of the many different ingredients can blend together in a savory mix.

Norma had Palestinian ancestry, as evidenced by her last name, Elías. Her husband, Juan—who spent weekdays in San Antonio de los Cobres, an old copper-mining town farther up in the mountains where he worked as a schoolteacher—was of Indigenous Qulla descent; his parents and grandparents before him all hailed from the Indigenous groups of the Puna, the Jujuy and Salta highlands. Sitting around the table were Norma's two sons, Gonzalo and Juan Gabriel Farfán Elías, and their two cousins, Flor and Ana, who were visiting from other nearby towns.

I brought the bowl of locro up to my mouth and drank the broth, the steam enveloping my face and making my nose run. Every few minutes at the table I applied Mentisan, a minty-smelling Bolivian ointment, to the outsides of my nostrils, refreshed by the slight burning sensation that quickly drained my sinuses and cleared up my congestion. It was the first thing that Norma offered me when she heard me enter her house sniffling. The cousins Gonzalo and Juan Gabriel and Flor and Ana, on the other hand, taught me how to chew coca leaves—a common practice in the region to combat headaches and other ailments mostly brought on by altitude sickness. I hesitantly placed several of the small green leaves in my cheek. As instructed, I used my tongue to press the leaves up against the inside of my mouth, to get the essence flowing. Soon enough, my tongue became numb and my cheek tingled.

"Does it taste like anything?" Flor asked.

I widened my eyes and jittered sarcastically. Everyone laughed. They insisted I carry a ziplock packet of coca leaves with me for the rest of my travels in the northwest, in case I needed it. I neatly folded the clear pouch and put it in my backpack, careful to ensure that no stray leaves would fall out and come back to haunt me at customs in New York several weeks later.

We ate and we laughed some more. The family noticed my Argentine accent—which had grown stronger over the course of the past month or so—and, wanting me to pick up some new slang, they taught me how to curse. They would say a word and explain its meaning. I would repeat it, and we would all cackle with delight. But the most enjoyable part of our evening together came when we sat passing a guitar around, trading songs. I would play popular tunes in English, to which everyone knew the words. In exchange, the Farfán brothers, a professional folk music duo, played songs from the different folkloric traditions of the Argentine northwest: romantic zambas, energetic chacareras, and bailecitos, which feature guitars and pan flutes. They sang of the Pachamama, Mother Earth, the ancient Incan goddess that people still worshipped across the Andes. One song, written by the Argentine folk legend Atahualpa Yupanqui, had a refrain that I would not soon forget: "Para el que mira sin ver, la Tierra es tierra no más." For the person who looks without seeing, the Earth is land and nothing more.

Gonzalo sang and Juan Gabriel played a wide-body guitar with nylon strings. Together they frequented fairs and festivals across the Andes. Musical instruments were scattered about their house: guitars upon guitars, drums and keyboards and pan flutes, and a ronroco—a traditional Andean instrument about the size of a ukulele with a high-pitched twang of a sound—made from the spiny shell of an armadillo. At one point Gonzalo began to sing a song of his own, which was called "Quijano me voy" (I'm Headed to Quijano). "Quijano me voy" is a slow zamba. The studio version features a constant blend of worlds old and new: the melancholy bandoneon, of twentieth-century tango fame, sets a tremendously nostalgic tone above the age-old strumming and deft finger-picking, fixtures of Argentina's Indigenous musical traditions of the interior. But here, in the quiet of their home, the wind blowing viciously outside in the cold, it was just the brothers and a guitar as they sang this simple, poetic elegy for their beloved hometown, a love song to their land. It began with a spoken refrain: "To your mountains and canyons / to your wandering streams / I sing this glowing song in homage / to my dear portal of the Andes . . ."

Gonzalo sang about Campo Quijano as a place often longed for, a place where the one who has left always hopes to someday return, so that their dreams might at last come true. In a way, the town's very name evoked such a sense of hope and yearning: the Spanish folk hero Alonso Quijano, more often known as Don Quixote, is famous for his own romantic dreams and idealized adventures. It made sense, too, that these brothers, sons of an Indigenous Qulla father and an Argentine-born Palestinian mother, were so attuned to notions of home and belonging, having hailed from communities historically displaced. Seemingly, they channeled that loss into a fervent love for the place where they were born.

Hours passed in this way and eventually, our voices hoarse

from so much singing, it was time for bed. A family of school-teachers and folk singers, their home was humble: the girls slept with Norma in one bedroom, and us boys slept in another. We said goodnight. I tucked myself in under several layers of warm wool and flannel blankets and wedged a rubber hot-water bottle between my legs.

I lay there restless for a few minutes, thinking. Did it matter if Selim Salama actually did all the things that he said? Why did I really come to the Andes, to Argentina, all alone like this? I remembered what the historian María Cherro de Azar had told me in her apartment back in Buenos Aires. *In their travels on the train and on the road, the turcos learned things.* Her words, seeming almost prophetic now, echoed in my mind. *They made friends . . . They sang, they danced tangos, they heard the folk music of the Andes for the first time. They became fluent in Spanish. They became Argentine . . .*

What is a home if not a place where the stories sound familiar?

Juan Gabriel and Gonzalo were breathing heavily, fast asleep, and I remembered the days when, as a child, I shared a single room like this with both of my younger brothers: each of us in a twin bed, filling the space with the heat that radiated from our bodies as we slept, a single unit against the cold, hard wind outside.

La Quiaca (Argentina) – Villazón (Bolivia)

THE CROSSING INTO BOLIVIA WAS AT LA QUIACA, an Argentine border town situated along a riverbed at a dizzying eleven thousand feet above sea level. La Quiaca is the northern terminus of both Ruta 40—3,227 miles away from its southernmost point, in Patagonia—and Ruta 9, two historic trading roads that have since become busy highways filled with trucks, cars, and long-distance coach buses.

Throughout my quixotic journey, Bolivia had occupied something of a more distant space in my imagination. It was a place I was unsure my great-grandfather had ever reached, the border a line I wasn't sure he'd ever actually crossed, so in some ways I was never fully convinced that I would make it there myself. Now here I was. Though I'd been feeling rather dejected about the idea that the trail of the Lost Salamas had gone cold for good, I figured that since I'd made it this far, I should at least cross the border.

Bolivia, whose many different Indigenous peoples have largely maintained their traditions and origins, is very different from Argentina, a nation completely transformed by immigration and colonialism. More than 60 percent of Bolivians identify as Indigenous, the largest proportion of any nation in the Americas. This part of Bolivia—in the southwest corner of a dazzlingly vast country of rainforests, highlands, and deserts—is a land of extremes. There were high plains and dramatic badlands, dark-red canyons and the blinding, endless salt flats of the Salar de Uyuni. In the town of San Vicente, close to the Argentine border, the American outlaws Butch Cassidy and Harry Longabaugh (better known as the Sundance Kid) were said to have been killed in a shootout in 1908. Farther north was mountainous Potosí, home to the largest silver mine in the history of the American continent.

The combination of its wild remoteness and concentration of mineral wealth gave the southern Bolivian altiplano an even more interesting atmosphere of trade and exchange as the twentieth century began. "Caravans began regular journeys into Bolivia bearing merchandise of cloth chiefly, besides important quantities of tea, spices, jewelry, and the costlier varieties of hardware," wrote the geographer Isaiah Bowman in his 1910 book *Trade Routes in the Economic Geography of Bolivia*, which discusses in detail the La Quiaca–Villazón border region. "For these were exchanged the silver, blankets, dried and hence light-weight potatoes, and the coca, of the mountain Indians." At the time of writing, Bowman continued, La Quiaca was also anticipating a rail line that would cross the border, connecting it with the Bolivian Antofagasta Railway—only three years earlier, in 1907, the General Manuel Belgrano Railway had reached the town from the south, linking La Quiaca with Jujuy and onward to Buenos Aires until passenger rail service was largely discontinued throughout Argentina in the second half of the twentieth century. By the time I got there, all that was left were the broken remnants of track, which snaked up and through the Quebrada de Humahuaca alongside the road.

But La Quiaca's land border with Villazón, its raucous Bolivian counterpart, remained an important point of transit and trade for both countries. Villazón itself, with its clogged roads and bustling stalls selling knockoff synthetic soccer jerseys and Indigenous fabrics alike, was a place where people came to buy things on the cheap. Argentines living in La Quiaca were able to cross by foot without clearing immigration for brief visits to the other side, but they were told that they could go no farther than Villazón or they would risk breaking the law. Everyone else had to wait in line.

I waited alongside dozens of present-day merchants who carried various items for sale. The men seemed to deal mostly in electronics, using wheelbarrows and metal carts to transfer heavier items like televisions. The women, almost all of whom wore black bowler hats and long woolen chola skirts, carried various produce and clothing items in large woven cloths called aguayos, wrapped tightly around their backs. Others, instead of carrying merchandise, carried children, who sat in these multicolored aguayos as though they were miniature hammocks. It seemed precarious, this method of transportation: the women moving quickly down the street, the infants and small toddlers swinging behind them as they walked.

I asked one of the women in line next to me why she carried her child like this.

"If I hold him to my chest, he will look at nothing but his mother," she told me. "This way, at least he can see the world I've passed through."

———

The crossing itself was a bridge over a wide, dry riverbed. A Bolivian family, standing beside a Jeep a few dozen meters to the east of the bridge, was washing clothes in the trickle of a creek that was all that existed, for now, of the Río de la Quiaca. We were held up by passengers from a transnational coach bus completing its border crossing. It had arrived from Quito, Ecuador; traversed all of Peru and Bolivia; and was bound for Buenos Aires, at this point at least another full day's land journey away. The travelers looked visibly tired as they shuffled through customs. I couldn't help but find myself fascinated by how far they'd come. At airports I can stare at the departures screens forever, mesmerized by the lists of destinations, which change with each city or country. But airplanes feel unnatural—like traveling through time and space without a sense of where you are. At Villazón's bus terminal, according to the signs and schedules posted, I could board a single coach and hours or days later be in La Paz, or Lima, or Bogotá. Instead, I hopped onto a northbound rapidito, a minivan shared by six passengers, bound for a town less than two hours north called Tupiza.

In Bolivia the sky was endless, a deep, dark blue. We shot across the burning desert, leaving behind trails of dust fading quickly in our wake. Clusters of adobe homes huddled together amid the bleak expanse of altiplano, as if finding strength in numbers so as not to be absorbed by the vastness that surrounded them. The people who lived in these communities hitched rides in rapiditos and on the backs of pickup trucks. The road ahead of us undulated like a transverse wave on this high plain, rising and falling with the ground beneath it. A cluster of policemen waited on the crest of one of these hills, able to focus their radar on speeding vehicles several miles away. Our driver groaned, realizing his mistake out of the corner of his eye while zooming downhill; a few minutes later, we reached the officers, who had already blocked off the road. The driver pulled over and immediately exited the car with his attendant. Their negotiations, which I watched out my window, lasted just five minutes. A few bills were handed off to the police, and we were once again on our way.

During one such descent, the road veered to the right, in front of a small rocky mound that blocked our view of what was ahead. As we circumvented the mound, the land in front of us suddenly opened to an otherworldly valley below filled with amber outcrops and jagged badlands like teeth in the depths. I watched out the window as the van veered far too close to the cliff's edge with every turn. An elderly man sitting next to me crossed his heart in silent prayer. I remembered one of Selim Salama's favorite stories, as told by his now-elderly grandson Rulo, in which he claimed to have convinced a fellow salesman to jump off a moving train with him just seconds before it derailed and careened off the edge of a mountain, killing everyone on board. It was a purely impossible story—I now knew as much. Scouring Argentine and Bolivian historical records, I found no record of any train crashes in the region as dramatic and fatal as the kind that Selim Salama described.

The land around Tupiza was stunning—high-altitude desert marked by narrow cactus-strewn quebradas that widened into vast canyons of red rock. A guide named Juan took me on a Jeep ride along dried-out riverbed roads, ancient trade routes once frequented by caravans of merchants and pack animals. Now we passed day-laborers crowding into pickup trucks bound for the metal mines, and women commanding large herds of llama, sheep, and goats. But after two restless nights alone in town, I felt the urge to return to Argentina.

I went back to La Quiaca to spend some time with two storytellers: a radio journalist named Silvia Martínez and a Quechua historian and folklorist named Laura Cruz. Silvia and I wandered the cold and windy streets for a few hours, looking for the few remaining Middle Eastern families who had stores in the town. A large man named Miguel Chehadi owned a general store that sold canned foods and bottles of beer on a quiet corner. On his counter were three flags: Argentina, Bolivia, and Syria. The Syrian history of La Quiaca, Silvia told me, was older than the town itself (which was founded in 1907). Around 1900, the first Ottoman Christians reached the border settlement, then just another cluster of homes near the river, to sell soap and clothes to the miners and the herders working in these highlands. Further waves continued well into the twentieth century, after the Ottoman Empire's dissolution and even into the reign of the Assad family.

"I'd like it if you came to my house later this afternoon, so that you can understand the full importance of the story you are telling," Silvia told me.

Silvia's apartment, on a quiet block set back from the center of town, was in the midst of a complete renovation. Paint and sheetrock had been stripped from the walls. Everyday items from her dismantled shelves were piled atop the furniture and strewn about the floors. If she hadn't told me any different, I would have assumed that the building was being constructed anew. "I'm sorry for the mess," Silvia said, stepping over several cats and potted plants as we made our way through the entrance. She was a small woman in her early sixties with short, gray hair, the descendant of Spanish and Palestinian Christian ancestors. Laura Cruz, the Quechua historian and professor, was sitting at a small table in the kitchen, sipping mate.

Together, they wanted to tell me about their town's Day of the Dead celebration. "Celebrated each November second," Laura said, "here it's called the Culto a los Muertos." It is a day of remembrance, not just for the most recently deceased but for all those ancestors who live on in the memories of their descendants. Jewish tradition calls for such remembrances on the anniversary of each relative's death; in the Roman Catholic tradition, on All Souls' Day, the departed are remembered and respected all at once.

Central to the celebration is the act of baking bread, which is provided as an offering to the deceased. In every region of the Americas, this is done differently: in the northernmost highlands of Argentina, the dough is molded into shapes resembling humans, fish, llamas, and dogs. The tradition dates back hundreds of years, but in many of the more isolated Andean towns where wheat is not cultivated, flour was scarcely available until as recently as the mid-twentieth century. The inhabitants of the altiplano and the Puna relied on turcos—coming from more fertile areas in the south and east like Mendoza, San Juan, and the Pampas—to bring the necessary ingredient to towns that needed it. "When the turco brought bread or flour, it was like a miracle," María Cherro de Azar had told me about the Syrian Jewish peddlers in the Andes.

Their arrival was often so anticipated that the human-shaped bread dolls have become known colloquially in La Quiaca as *turcos* ever since. They're decorated with large mustaches and bushy black eyebrows—physical features of men from Arab lands that were noted by the native peoples of the Andes, who in general do not grow much facial hair. The turcos, in bread form, are presented as offerings to reconnect the dead with the living.

Several days before the Day of the Dead is another festival that has been held at the end of each October for more than a century in order to provide a venue for these important transactions. Since the late nineteenth century, hundreds of artisans from southern Bolivia and the northern Andes of Argentina and Chile converge on La Quiaca with clay pots, terra-cotta plates, and other handmade pottery to exchange for desirable products brought from other regions and climates. In Quechua the word for these pots is *manka*, and so the blended Quechua-Spanish name for the event has long been Manka Fiesta. It remains popular, though in a globalized world of industrial shipping and the constant movement of goods, the event is more ceremonial nowadays. Historically, the Manka Fiesta played a vital role for many otherwise-isolated communities, attracting merchants from across Argentina and Bolivia. In the first half of the twentieth century, especially, the turcos were major players, arriving with popular merchandise such as cotton clothes, which were more versatile than llama wool. Others brought foodstuffs beyond just the aforementioned bread and flour; I thought of the Daruich brothers and Claudio Cruz Caqui, whose carts of cured meats and colorful sweets frequented the vast river valleys and lonely highland roads.

Cash was rarely exchanged at the Manka Fiesta. Bartering was more common, and many of the merchants most likely resold the pottery on their return journeys home. "Our ancestors probably did business together," Laura and Silvia concluded. Silvia stood up, walked over to her kitchen cabinet, and pulled out a manka, which she said was mine to keep. It was a water jug, taller than it was wide, clay-colored like so many of the homes in town, and painted with a strip of fine-stenciled drawings of animals and plants. Manka, they explained, also served another purpose. Long ago, artistic depictions like these were used to pass down legends and oral histories of the Andes, stories etched in clay.

"Are you sure?" I said quietly, taking the manka in my hands. It was rough, not glazed or smooth, and it made a scraping noise when I rubbed it with my finger. Suddenly I found myself apologizing to the two women. "I'm sorry, I have nothing to give in return."

Laura smiled. "You have a story." By keeping the tale of my great-grandfather alive, she continued, it meant that their ancestors' stories would be kept alive, too.

"Take it," Silvia said. "You're a turco."

Hola Abuelo,

I'm learning that people tell stories in all kinds of
ways. Through songs, through crafts, through
everyday items. Today, I made a trade with two
women on the border with Bolivia. All I had to offer
was the story of my journey from Mendoza, and of
our family, and it was enough for them. In return
they gave me a clay pot with drawings on the side.

After that I started to think: What if the Lost
Salamas aren't really children after all?

What if they are traces of another kind, the origins
of an identity, a story that you have always known
but that I am just beginning to understand?

I'm leaving the Andes tonight. There are a few more
places where I think I need to go.

Jordan

Patagonia

DRIVE DOWN THE LONG GRAVEL ROADS OF THE
Península Valdés and you can see cars coming up behind you
from many miles away in your rearview mirror. They look
like mini tornadoes kicking up dust as they race through the
lonely Patagonian steppe. Península Valdés is characterized
by an almost unfathomable emptiness, different from the Patagonia of the southern Andes, where mountains harboring
ice-blue glacial lakes and dark-green pine forests loom over
you like in a postcard. The Patagonia of Península Valdés is
flat and virtually barren, with foot-high shrubs and endless
visibility. No planes fly overhead; there are hardly any buildings. At night the brown landscape plunges into darkness and
silence. The coast offers the only respite from this desolation.
Wildlife abounds where the sheer cliffs meet crystalline coves
and the open Atlantic. Elephant seals muscle in on Magel-
lanic penguins, and southern right whales comb the frigid,
turquoise waters alongside orcas.

Every time I'd sought physical traces of my great-grandfather,
I'd come up short. Yet I was discovering that it was far more
rewarding to live in the spirit of the turcos' wanderings. The
conversation with the bombilla salesman, the Manka Fiesta,

the tastes of Syria in the Andes—these encounters connected me to my heritage much more clearly than a distant biological link with a stranger ever could have. And so in another season, another time, I came south to Patagonia, thousands of miles from Selim Salama's actual trade route, for a very specific reason: I wanted to meet a gaucho. Argentina's famous mestizo horsemen were prominent in the stories Middle Eastern immigrants told of their time on the road. Arising in the eighteenth and nineteenth centuries as nomads, gauchos once roamed freely about the north-central Pampas; they hunted abundant free-grazing cattle, sheep, and horses for meat and hides, and set up simple camps at night in the grasslands. The word *gaucho* is most commonly thought to be derived from versions of *guacho*, a Guaraní and Quechua term that literally means "orphan," or "one who is born without a known father." Like much else in the Argentine collective memory and imagination, the gaucho as a figure almost always evokes feelings of melancholy and longing.

"Los gauchos," wrote Mariano Florencio Grondona in an essay for the newspaper *La Nación*, "were only possible in a natural world that no longer exists. They were born in a vast land of never-ending pastures, where wild cattle roamed without wire fences blocking their way and without owners who prohibited their capture." Having played a crucial role in the independence wars against the Spanish colonizers in the 1810s and 1820s, gauchos were known to be fearsome fighters, talented horseback riders, and remarkable storytellers. Exactly the kind of figure who would have appealed to Selim Salama, I thought. "In this world of nature," Grondona continued, "the gaucho lived his romance."

As the nineteenth century wore on, however, the land on which they relied was increasingly divided and fenced off into private estancias for industrial-scale agriculture. The deflated gauchos, still more skilled than anyone else as horsemen and cowboys, were relegated to working as farmhands. Those who did not settle were pushed to the frontiers—Patagonia and the Andes—and treated like fugitive outlaws. According to Grondona, "The gaucho was no longer the same on foot. He went from king to peon."

Yet by the turn of the twentieth century, the figure of the gaucho—who now existed somewhere in between the free-wheeling transitory lifestyle of the settlers' forefathers and the more sedentary, capitalist ranching life of the present—also became emblematic of the identity crisis of a rapidly changing nation. Due to immigration from Europe and the Middle East, Argentina was in the midst of a population boom. By 1910, one out of every three Argentines was an immigrant. New railroad lines were built and existing ones were extended. The agricultural industry was modernized for an export economy. Indigenous people were increasingly displaced from their ancestral lands. "The figure of the gaucho thus came to embody the unresolved question of national identity," wrote Edwin Williamson in his biography of Jorge Luis Borges, Argentina's most celebrated writer, whose work often included gaucho characters and themes. "A question that would gnaw away at the Argentine conscience and would resurface periodically in a violent impulse to hold on to or retrieve some vital essence that might be lost as Argentina acquired the trappings of a modern nation."

Though likely to be revered forever in Argentine national memory, gaucho culture in practice is headed rapidly toward extinction. Motorized farm equipment has largely replaced horses, agricultural technologies have become more efficient, science has offered explanations for even the most confounding of country legends, and the horsemen's traditions are now more easily observed in demonstrations for tourists on luxury estancias than in the once-freewheeling grasslands.

Laura Ferro is a thirty-four-year-old photographer trying to document the old ways of the gauchos before they disappear for good. Her family has been herding sheep on Península Valdés ever since her great-grandfather migrated from Italy to Argentina in 1888. As a young girl, she would fall asleep to the eerie songs of distant whales and hear stories of the lonely gauchos who roamed the steppe. She became so completely enraptured by the history and nature of Argentina's great Patagonian peninsula that as an adult she set out to document as much of it as she could.

"This is a place where the past lives on all around you," Laura told me one morning over breakfast in Puerto Pirámides, the only town on the peninsula. "It lives on in fossils that are thirty million years old, in megalodon teeth, in old tools, in sharpened stones. In the landscape itself. I am obsessed with visualizing the passage of time." She pulled out a book of hers called *El tiempo es un paisaje* (Time is a Landscape), for which she roamed the peninsula and attempted to reconstruct a trove of black-and-white photographs taken by an unknown visitor to the region at the turn of the twentieth century. She took each one from the same position, even going as far as to wait for the same wind and weather conditions, in order to show the old and new renderings side by side. The many similarities that remained left the few differences exposed. In one of Laura's photos, a natural stone pyramid that once served as the namesake of the village where we sat had crumbled and disappeared. In others, coastal erosion was clear. Despite the changes in the physical landscape, the photos were remarkable reconstructions. "I'm always reconstructing, always reconstructing," she said.

Her impulse to wander and document a vanishing world close to her family's past arose from a situation remarkably similar to my own. Her late grandfather, a man named Emilio Ferro, kept an impressive library. His study, in the main house of the grand estancia that still belongs to the family, was lined with dark-wood cabinets filled with leather-bound volumes of geological and botanical surveys of the region, huge framed maps from centuries past, and old photos of her great-grandfather and his gaucho companions camping out in the fields. In a nearby wooden shed on the property, a creaky door opened to reveal dressers stuffed with more old papers, journals, and ledgers than anyone other than Laura knew what to do with. "I began collecting fossils, classifying maps, arranging photos, drawings, letters, and travel diaries," she wrote in the book. "As the archaeologist of our family archives, I was reconstructing my own story."

Her family owned a third of the peninsula's land, and still operated a thriving wool business. They employed around half a dozen gauchos, she said. Perhaps I could stay with someone that night.

A burly, young-looking man with red hair was in charge of managing the family's peninsula properties. His name was Juan Castro. We awoke him from a nap when we stopped by his cabin in the heat of the mid-afternoon.

"We've got a young peon out by La Caleta." Juan Castro

yawned as he spoke. La Caleta was a distant, solitary cove on the eastern edge of the peninsula, forty miles from town on washboard roads through the middle of nowhere. "He's only been there for a few months, but you can stay the night with him if you want."

"Really?" I asked.

"Yes, of course." He spoke nonchalantly, as though he were offering me a glass of water.

"Should I bring any sort of gift?"

"No gift, no worries. Maybe he will make an asado and you can eat that, though." At the mention of this, Laura's eyes widened. I could tell that, like me, she was someone held captive by the enchantments of the past. "You have something to write on?" Juan Castro continued. I pulled out my notepad and a pen. He took them into his thick hands and started writing something down. "There's no signal out there. Show him this, and you're good to go." He handed back the notepad, and I looked at what he had written:

PEREIRA.

JORDAN IS GOING TO SLEEP WITH YOU TONIGHT IN LA CALETA. LET HIM IN. MAKE HIM COMFORTABLE.

I AM JUAN CASTRO.

I was to arrive before sundown, Juan Castro instructed. I thanked him profusely and he returned to his room without saying much else.

"Listen," Laura warned me in the car as we pulled away, "I just want to make sure you know, it's going to be pretty rustic, eh."

————

The sun was low, and the light was growing long across the land when I pulled up to the gaucho's outpost, which consisted of a few small brick structures with tin roofs beside an old sheep-shearing barn. Everything was silent but for the whipping wind and the faint sound of waves lapping against a nearby cove. Nothing, nobody was there. I made my way down a small hill behind the brick houses and found a campsite littered with sheep carcasses, woolskins, and a recently abandoned fire pit that still smelled of the previous night's embers.

In the golden days of the grasslands and the steppe, the campfire was close to sacred for gauchos and other wanderers— a place where anyone out in the lonely country who spotted its orange glow could gather for a warm rest and lively conversation over mate. Its perimeter was demarcated by horse bones, or by half-buried coals, or by bricks made of adobe or clay. Those who arrived would be offered food: meat grilled over the open flame, maybe some eggs (of rheas and ducks and coots) and corn on the cob.

The campfire was not only a place to eat and drink but also a venue where business could be settled and other issues of serious importance discussed: potential conflicts, new dangers, recent ambushes nearby. The colder the weather, the more crowded the gatherings, and the taller the tales. The culture of the gauchos—and that of the Argentine countryside more generally, I'd learned in the Andes—was deeply rooted in these traditions of oral history and storytelling. Often these stories took the form of dueling payadas, or battles of verse, narrated in the décima rhythm to emulate the sound of a galloping horse: da-DA, da-DA, da-DA, da-DA. The reply to one story was always the start of another. There were classic folktales—myths, and legends from life on the road and in the fields. There were accounts of the most famous gauchos mythologized as heroes, wrote the author Horacio Ortiz, "similar to Hercules or Samson, but of the knife, the poncho, and the chiripá." But it was just as common to tell fantastic, impossible stories with oneself as the protagonist—stories of riding and fighting skills, of exploits of passion and desire. These stories, of course, could never be proven. Perhaps that was part of the point. It sounded all too familiar: da-DA, da-DA, da-DA, da-DA.

The stories grew darker with the night. There were apparitions, revenants, ghosts. "Watch out for the Luz Mala," I could imagine Selim Salama telling his children before they went to bed in Buenos Aires, many years after his adventures in the countryside. The Evil Light—or the will-o'-the-wisp, as it is most often known in English—was so terrifying that it made even the hardiest of men shake with fright. Thought to mark the presence of a lost and sorrowed soul, the ghastly atmospheric light would appear late at night in mountain passes or out in the open country over swamps and fields, often leading travelers astray. Some said it marked the location of bountiful treasure, never to be found, and in other contexts, the idea of the will-o'-the-wisp alone has come to represent a hope or a goal that is impossible to achieve.

In fact, the bioluminescence is the result of gases released by bones and other organic matter in decomposition. But don't all tall tales exist to make some sense of the real world? Aren't all fabulous stories rooted somewhat in truth?

Those days were all but gone now, and all that seemed to be left were these pits of ash and burnt wood, vestiges of decades and centuries past. I couldn't help but think it made sense that I was alone here. I wondered where I would go—what I would do—if no one showed up. Night would soon fall. There was no phone service for dozens of miles. Puerto Pirámides was a long forty miles away and my small rented sedan likely wouldn't be able to survive the rough roads in the dark, not to mention the guanacos and the rheas dashing out of the shadows. A bit farther up the road from here was a ranger station, where a guardafauna named Natalia spent ten-day shifts watching for orcas from her perch atop a tall cliff. Península Valdés is famous, in part, because it is one of the few places on Earth where the orcas beach themselves to hunt seals on the shore, lunging viciously toward land with the crashing waves before pulling their prey with them back into the sea.

Far across the way, after many miles of steppe, I could make out another ranching outpost, but I couldn't be sure that it was occupied. At that moment I was struck by the familiarity of my situation: it was not lost on me that in seeking such company I had presented myself with some of the same solitary decisions that my great-grandfather, and many itinerant merchants of decades past, would have potentially encountered on the road. Of course, my context was still vastly different: I had extra food in my backpack, I had a cell phone (though it had no signal), I had warm clothes. I could always sleep in the car and drive back to town the next morning, rather defeated but nonetheless unscathed. Even seventy-five years earlier, that would have hardly been an option. Selim Salama, alone in the northwestern Andes of the 1920s, would have faced challenges, natural and human, unlike any other he had experienced before. Traveling salesmen of the time were forced to adapt to the whims of the road—eating what they were offered or the little that they could scavenge from the farms and the field, and sleeping anywhere they were given shelter.

I sat down and waited for a while, and I let my mind wander. I recalled a conversation I'd had just a few days earlier with a ninety-year-old Argentine newspaperman named Ricardo Biglieri. From Buenos Aires, I was supposed to drive to visit Biglieri at his home in Pergamino, a farming town some two hours northwest of the capital, where he'd lived all his life. But on the morning of our planned meeting, the old writer called to tell me he wasn't feeling well, and suggested we speak by phone instead.

"I have terrible laryngitis!" Biglieri shouted very hoarsely on the other end of the line. Even without intact vocal cords, the writer spoke with a formidable, high-pitched gusto. He conveyed his thoughts in the kind of deeply poetic Spanish expressions that are difficult to replicate in English. When I told him my age, he let out a loud shriek. "AHHH!" he exclaimed, and I imagined him wildly waving his arms. "Estás en la flor de la juventud!" *You're in the flower of youth*, the old man had said. "Enjoy it," he continued. "These days, it's hard for me just to get out of bed."

What Biglieri said he lacked in physical faculties, he made up for with an encyclopedic memory and a vast wealth of stories from his childhood: he grew up on a pig farm on the very outskirts of central Pergamino and wrote often about 1930s and 1940s life in the Pampas, those famously vast fertile plains that stretch from the Atlantic to the Andes in the central part of the country. I found my way to him because, years ago, he'd written one blog post for an Argentine folklore website that told the story of a Middle Eastern traveling salesman who passed frequently by his family's farm in the late 1930s, when Biglieri was hardly ten years old. No one knew the young merchant's real name, but everyone called him El Turco Mata.

"I was entranced by all that he brought with him in his little carriage," Biglieri recalled. El Turco Mata rode a horse-drawn cart; other hamleros, especially in the earliest years of the twentieth century, journeyed on foot, with poles across their shoulders, burlap sacks hanging from each end. El Turco Mata carried an array of physical merchandise for sale—from clothes, home goods, and hardware to dried meats and sweets—but in other ways, too, the man was a roving novelty, a mixed bag of surprises. "He knew enough to prepare Turkish delicacies for us," Biglieri said. Here he continued to use the word *turco*, Turkish, to mean Middle Eastern. "He brought special Turkish grains and kneaded them into dough."

From the town center of Pergamino, where the young peddler was said to have a house and a family, it was nearly thirty miles to the Biglieri family farm, and then another thirty to forty miles more to the end of his route. Without an automobile, El Turco Mata had no choice but to sleep at the ranches and the outposts of the people he served in the countryside. "He sat at our table; he slept in our home," Biglieri told me. "We so looked forward to his visits."

Biglieri wasn't sure what El Turco Mata's religion was, but he knew that the peddler wasn't Catholic like his family. "Something Ottoman, I think," he said. And then the old man made a particularly curious and illuminative comment in passing: "We called him 'cazarino,' hunter—a joke because he was oddly fond of dairy," Biglieri said. "He rarely ever ate meat in our house."

Being Jewish is like this. We are a people who constantly question and adapt, and only ever are we able to move forward if we modify our traditions and laws and customs in a way that is reasonable, livable for us wherever we are. For my family, and indeed for many families I know, these kinds of modifications are as old as time. "My grandfather [Selim Salama] used to make us grandchildren turn on the television for him during Shabbat," said my father's older cousin Coco in Mexico. The old man still prayed every morning at Or Torah because that is what his community expected. He wrapped tefillin and made b'nei mitzvah for his children and implored them to marry Jewish partners so that the family's traditions would not be lost.

I do not consider myself religious, yet I maintain certain customs that are undoubtedly rooted in faith, especially when it comes to food. I won't eat bread during the eight days of Passover. I fast each year on Yom Kippur—or at least I try my best, because I've also often gone to work and to school on the holiday. I never pray, but I'm not sure I've ever intentionally taken a bite of pork. There are plenty of more observant Jews who will eat only vegetarian outside the house, so as to avoid meat that is not kosher; others won't eat any kind of food that is not kosher at all.

On the road, during reporting journeys, I have developed vague strategies around this most peculiar question of food, trying to remain polite while at the same time respecting my own customs and those of the kind people who allow me into their homes. "Delicious," I'll say to a hearty serving of stew. Then, curiously but casually, "What kind of meat is in it?"

We might do these things for any number of reasons, and everyone's reasons are different. Perhaps it is out of piety and the belief that it is necessary to adhere to the laws and codes of the faith, so as to be continually inscribed, one year after the next, in the Book of Life. Maybe it is because we are taught a certain set of values by our parents and our grandparents and by upholding those values in our lives, we are in turn validating them. Maybe, for a people comprising not 0.2 percent of the world's total population, it is a way for us to maintain our sense of difference, to feel that we belong to something larger than ourselves. Certainly for me it also comes from an understanding that many of our ancestors escaped where they lived in order to preserve these values and ways of life, and that many others did not make it out—that for us to continue now is out of respect for their sacrifices.

So we pick and choose in ways that may seem arbitrary to some but make perfect sense to others. Some of us will eat chicken parmigiana but not a cheeseburger. Others enjoy shrimp and shellfish but will not touch pork. Some of us are willing to pick bacon off a sandwich; others of us will feel we have no choice but to awkwardly send it back. Still others are willing to eat anything and everything. Many Jewish people who want to honor Shabbat, a day of rest, will drive to synagogue to do so, or ask our children to turn on the light switch, or use an elevator that stops at every floor so long as we do not have to operate it. These things may seem contradictory, but they are not hypocrisies. They are adaptations, little by little, so that we can keep our place in a world that has never accepted us.

Working and traveling in this way, my father slept where he could, he ate what was available (not kosher, of course), and he relieved himself in open fields, or in village outposts and cesspits, or along the road. On the windy steppe of Península Valdés, waiting for the gauchos to arrive, I remembered reading this in Abuelo's *Historia Antigua*, well before I ever knew I would set off myself on this long and fraught journey into a country I hardly knew. I wondered to what extent Selim Salama would have gone to avoid certain kinds of foods, if he prayed when no one was watching, how often he slept in the company of others, and how often he was otherwise left to spread out a burlap sack in the open air on the side of the trail.

Suddenly I heard the rumble of an engine, which interrupted my train of thought as though jolting me awake from a fever dream. I turned around to see a large dump truck careening down the road. Two men sat atop its load of cargo in the bed, and two more were in the cabin. They saw me but made little acknowledgment of my presence—no waves, only wary stares.

The men parked their truck next to my car in front of the

brick houses and turned off the engine. I said, "Pereira?" and one of them in the cabin nodded. He was thin, with jet-black hair and sad, tired eyes. I handed him Juan Castro's note. He read it and smiled. "Let's go in and talk," Pereira said.

The gauchos began unloading supplies right away: toilet paper, huge packages of yerba and flour, a couple of thin mattresses rolled up and tied with thick ropes. They were shepherds, in the business of wool. By day they tended to herds of sheep, making sure they were grazing in the right places and that their drinking wells were filled with water. In the bed of the truck there were also woolskins, hairy sleeping sheepdogs, and a huge raw cut of lamb, which I guessed to be our dinner.

Intentionally or not, these gauchos were maintaining customs and traditions that were hundreds of years old. As the gaucho figure became increasingly emblematic of the nation's identity, so too did his image. The Gaucho Martín Fierro, an epic poem penned in 1872 by the writer José Hernández about a gaucho displaced from his land, marginalized, and banished to the frontier, quickly became a seminal text in Argentine literature and helped produce an archetypal image of the gaucho, with his cup of mate, his boleadoras, and his round guitar. An ongoing debate questions how widespread these practices were among gauchos everywhere before the book was published, versus how many gauchos in fact adopted that image in order to conform to the depiction of the book's hero in real life.

But Pereira and his companions were traditionally dressed, wearing flatcaps (boinas), cotton pants (bombachas de campo), and soft espadrilles with wool socks. "More comfortable for horseback riding," said Pereira, shrugging off the idea that they were as interested in any kind of preservation as they were in practicality. "Jeans burn."

We went inside, and Pereira hung the lamb carcass on a hook in a wooden cupboard that faced the sea and was kept cool by the offshore breeze. It was the only form of refrigeration he had.

"Do you drink mate?" Manuel, one of the other gauchos, asked me.

"Yes, please."

We sat on benches around Pereira's long wooden table. "It's much too big for just me here, living alone," Pereira would later say of his one-room cabin, which to most anyone else would have seemed much too small. The whole place smelled very dank. In the back there was a latrine and a few washbasins. There was no running water. A garbage bag covered a broken window. In the corner of the room there was an old wood-burning furnace, and a propane stove for cooking. Adán, another of the shepherds, put water to heat in a tin kettle. Water for mate is best at just below the boiling point— any hotter and the loose green leaves will burn and taste too bitter. Adán tested the temperature of the water by pouring it over his finger onto the cement floor until it was to his liking.

Pereira quickly got to work mixing flour and water in a bowl for torta frita—salty, flat pieces of flavorless bread fried in a pot of thick oil and lamb fat. He rolled out the dough onto the table and cut it into square pieces. Once fried, it was yellow-white on the inside and crispy brown on the outside. From my bag, I took out some chocolates and pastries that I'd picked up on my way out of town. The men devoured them as they chatted. Adán and Manuel were the most talkative of the group. They spoke in a fast slang that was nearly impossible for me to understand. Pereira interjected every once in a while. The fourth gaucho was the quietest, and also the only one wearing a sweater and jeans. When he at last introduced himself, he told me his name was Abdul. "Árabe?" I asked, surprised, turning toward him. "Yes," he replied. "Turco." But he knew no more than that about where his family had come from.

When the last round of mate was finished, the other three gauchos announced they were leaving, each heading back to his own outpost to spend the next several solitary nights. In the absence of his companions, Pereira became more talkative. It seemed that he appreciated my company. Now twenty-seven years old, he told me he'd been living alone in the fields like this since he turned thirteen. "At first it was difficult. I missed home; I missed my family," he said. "But then, after a while, I got used to the silence. When you've got a lot on your mind, the silence helps sometimes."

"Helps you think," I offered.

"Or not think at all," Pereira replied.

Life with Pereira seemed transplanted from a century earlier. Meals were cooked in tin pots and pans and eaten on wooden tables and benches; provisions were stocked inside antique dressers falling apart, and in the winters log-burning furnaces were used to stave off the biting cold. Only a small solar panel, which powered a single lightbulb, belied these vestiges of the past. There were no television screens or smartphones—except for mine, which of course did not work, for there was no internet or cell phone signal, either.

At night, Pereira listened to the radio, a provincial station called Radio 3 that was one of the few AM signals that reached this far end of the peninsula. Each night, Pereira explained to me, the broadcaster read aloud messages for the solitary gauchos, "mensajes al poblador rural," sent in by family members trying to get in touch. The messages brought all sorts of news: requests of items for the men to bring when they next came home, or a planned time to make their way to a hilltop with faint cell service and expect a phone call. Even the AM signal was weak, and sometimes Pereira had to whack the side of his radio to get it to cooperate. "Mario, the family says that everyone is healthy and well," the broadcaster announced that night in one message, as the speakers crackled to life. Another message, later on, reported a wallet found with all of someone's important identification materials inside. Sometimes, in the saddest of cases, the radio is the only way a gaucho might learn of a death in the family and know to get back home in time for the funeral. Pereira said he never missed the show.

We listened to the broadcast over steaming hot bowls of puchero, a thick Argentine stew of meat and root vegetables, typical gaucho fare. Pereira had decided against an asado, but this was the next best thing. From his small cupboard, he took out the large cut of lamb, which had been slaughtered the day before, and began butchering it on the table. The multipurpose knife he used was long, with a wide blade that he sharpened daily on a stone and stored in a triangular leather sheath. "Every gaucho has his knife," Pereira said, and it served him for just about everything—food, animals, repairs. Rarely did he allow it to leave his sight. Six chunks of espinazo (vertebrae) went into the pot with chopped onions, potatoes, pumpkin, oregano, salt, and pepper. Pereira prepared the raw meat on the same surface where he cut the vegetables and where he'd rolled the dough for torta frita. "When the animal is truly fresh, it cooks faster in the boiling water," Pereira said. "That's why we boil the vegetables first, then add the meat. I put the onions in last, on top of the meat, and all the flavors melt down," he said. The potatoes, unpeeled, were caked with dirt as we tossed them into the scalding water.

When we finished eating, as if on a cue, he pulled out an acoustic guitar. "All of us who work the land, we're known as gauchos," Pereira said. "And every gaucho has his guitar." He began to play a sad-sounding song. "Aquí me pongo a cantar . . ." He recited from memory the famous first few lines from *The Gaucho Martín Fierro*. "Here I come to sing to the beat of my guitar: because a man who is kept from sleep by an uncommon sorrow comforts himself with singing, like a solitary bird."

He played milongas, folk music, and cumbias camperas. I asked Pereira why the songs all sounded so melancholy. "Because the life of the gaucho is solitary," he replied. "We're all human beings; we feel lonely, and sometimes there's no one to talk to. So what do we do? We sing." When he handed me the guitar and asked me if I knew how to play, I sang some American folk songs—"You Are My Sunshine" and "Goin' Across the Mountain" and "Red River Valley"—and when I roughly explained the Spanish translation of the lyrics, Pereira remarked on how similarly lonely they were. I told him that where I lived, people would do just about anything not to be lonely; that it was easy to feel like you were a part of nothing in the United States, even in the biggest cities or the friendliest towns. In Argentina I was starting to learn that much of what I did as a writer and a traveler—perhaps not unlike the turco traveling salesman—was about trying to find my place, and doing anything I could to seek a sense of belonging, too.

As much as I was enthralled by Pereira—by his peacefulness, by the majestic natural setting where he lived, by the reminder of an old, romanticized existence all but gone—I also couldn't help but compare his situation to that of many other landless campesinos working in difficult conditions across the American continent, from ranch hands in Colombia to coastal fishermen in Guatemala to strawberry pickers in the Salinas Valley of California. Did Pereira actually enjoy living like this, as he suggested? Of course, Pereira would never admit otherwise to me, but I wondered if a reverence for the figure of the legendary gaucho was putting off, inadvertently or not, important conversations around persisting class and caste inequality in rural Argentina. Laura Ferro's family seemingly felt the same: a year or so after I was there, they renovated all of the gauchos' outposts on their land, painting the walls and upgrading the facilities.

Before long, it was time to sleep. Pereira led me outside, under the cover of a million stars, to the other one-room brick building, which was filled with several twin beds. Each of us unfurled a dusty mattress onto a wooden frame. I asked Pereira why he didn't leave his bed in place each morning.

"The rats," he replied nonchalantly. "At least they don't carry disease."

We said goodnight. Pereira fell asleep almost immediately, his breathing steady and calm. It took me a while longer because I was distracted by the sound of eerie cries coming from the seashore. Every five seconds or so, these cries pierced the stillness. "Ahh!" They almost sounded like those of a terrified, injured man crying out helplessly. Counting them until I fell asleep, I waited until morning to ask what they were. Pereira told me they were the yelps of penguins.

———

The morning was cold and quiet. Refracted white sunlight streamed in through the small window. "It'll be cloudy all day," Pereira observed from his bed, and for a few minutes neither of us said another word. In silence we arose and packed up our mattresses. We stepped outside to find the entire world smothered in a heavy white fog. You could not see the ocean, just a couple hundred feet away. The ground was damp with dew. Back at the main house, Pereira put on a kettle of hot water, and we shared some mate and gulped down some cold leftover slices of fried bread.

"I probably won't go out today," the gaucho said softly. "No, I won't go out today at all. I'll stay in and clean, bake a loaf of bread, sleep a bit. The fog makes the world seem vast and more confusing."

I told Pereira that I'd better be going. "Very well." He nodded quietly. He looked slightly sad. I was welcome to stay for as long as I wanted, he said, but it was probably for the best. His supervisor Juan Castro would be coming soon with questions about the herds of sheep and the state of their drinking wells, things that were hardly any business of mine.

Later that night, a roaring coastal thunderstorm would sweep across the land; the little apartment where I was staying back in town would shake with the wind, and heavy drops of rain would pelt the windows like a hail of gunfire. But as I stepped outside Pereira's place to leave, the morning fog was still thick. Everything was so immensely quiet, the little brick house so still on the edge of a cliff by the sea, that you'd be hard-pressed to believe that anyone lived there at all. "Don't forget," Pereira said, handing me the slip of paper that had served as my passage to his outpost the day before. Still today I can tell you where that slip of paper is, tucked into one of my notebooks.

Buenos Aires

THE CARETAKER OF THE WALLED-IN SYRIAN JEWISH cemetery in Lomas de Zamora was an old man with white hair named Basilio Rueda. I knocked loudly on the tall metal doors, and after a few minutes he unlocked them and poked his head outside. He was wearing a button-down shirt and work pants riddled with holes. "I'm sorry," Basilio said, "but we're closed."

"My great-grandparents are buried here," I told the caretaker. "I came all the way from New York and I won't be here for much longer. Would it be alright if I took a look around?"

With that, he let me pass without hesitation. Lomas was unlike any graveyard I'd seen before, a miniature city with a skyline of glossy marble tombs that rested atop the cement pavement. Basilio, an evangelical Christian, lived here with his wife in a small house on the southern corner. Sunlight glinted off the dark slabs of stone, and so the air that hung over the cemetery was far warmer than on the other side of the gate. Two little girls, presumably Basilio's granddaughters, were running and skipping through the narrow corridors between the tombstones, laughing and playing.

"Do you know where they are, or do you need to use the book?"

It took me a moment to remember that Basilio was referring to my ancestors—people who were gone long before I was even born, people whose names I hadn't even known until just a short while before.

"The book, please," I replied. He took me into the office, where the room was lined with hundreds of little golden candles. If I wanted to, Basilio said, I could recite a Hebrew prayer that I did not understand, and light a candle in their memory. As I did, Basilio took out a large pile of neatly stacked white papers from a drawer. It was a directory. Each page contained a long alphabetical list of the interred, their personal details, and their location in the graveyard. One by one, I told him the names of my relatives and he marked down their details with a pencil on a small index card:

Name	Death Date	Birth Date
Selim (Salomon) Salama	8/31/1960	10/18/1886
Faride (Florinda) Cohen Hop de Salama	5/15/1969	3/19/1891
Jacobo Cohen Hop	9/22/1947	unknown
Sara Sabán de Cohen Hop	7/20/1954	c. 1868–69

When he was finished, Basilio took me to visit them. We passed names on headstones that I now recognized: Muhafra, Laham, Suli. There was the tomb of my great-great-grandmother Sara Sabán de Cohen Hop—mother of Faride Cohen Hop de Salama and grandmother of Abuelo—marked by a faded photo of her smoking a narghile that she brought from Ottoman Syria and never let out of her sight. The same hookah pipe sits on my grandparents' living room shelf in New York today, weighed down with salt. The grave of her husband, my great-great-grandfather, a blind baker named Jacobo Cohen Hop, was so old that neither the photo nor the inscription on his tombstone were visible. Today hardly anyone remained who remembered anything about him, except that he was so pious that he died of a heart attack while walking to synagogue in his very old age. The two Jacobos named for him now gone, I grew sad wondering how much time was left before his name would be completely forgotten, too.

Just as the heat of the sun reflecting off the tombstones was becoming almost unbearable, we reached the final resting place of my great-grandfather, Selim Salama ibn Huedaie, Abu Daoud. Memorialized across the generations as both Simón and Salomón (depending on who believed what story), and known in Hebrew as Shlomo, his tombstone was inscribed, once and for all, SALOMON SALAMA.

"He's very difficult to identify," I remarked aloud.

"He's right here," said Basilio, and he pointed again to the corresponding tomb.

It was hard to believe that I was finally standing over the physical remains of this ancestor that no one seemed to properly understand—this person who inhabited so many worlds that seemed to disappear almost as soon as he left them. It dawned on me that an outside observer might suggest that, despite all the searching I did in the farthest corners of this country and others, the only palpable evidence I had of the man's existence was right below me in the ground. He was born in Damascus's Haret al-Yahud, made it by boat to the mean streets of 1910s Buenos Aires, wandered about the Andes for six years in the roaring twenties, only to end up right here, with all the rest of his companions.

A few minutes later I was sitting with Basilio back in the office, and I asked the old man how he came to be the caretaker of the Jewish cemetery in Lomas de Zamora.

As it turns out, Basilio was born in the Andes—in Cafayate, the town of Walter Daruich and his wine shop, set among citrus orchards and vineyards and wide valleys. "I was a maestro panadero," an excellent baker, he said. In those days, the Argentine northwest was filled with Syrian Jewish families, and he worked for one of them.

"The turcos, they lived in a different world." Basilio chuckled. "We didn't know what they were. We used to call them 'gitanos.'" Only after he came to work for them and recognized newly familiar names did he at last realize that many of them must have been Arab Jews. I asked him if he remembered anything about the traveling salesmen who passed through Cafayate when he was young. He nodded emphatically. "The roads were dirt in those days, but they didn't let that stop them." They were everywhere, reaching even the remotest of towns.

"Because of all that," Basilio continued, almost as a passing thought, "there are loads of people with unknown fathers up there." Indeed, he explained, he was one of them: his last name, Rueda, which meant "wheel" in Spanish, was actually his mother's surname. He never met his father. Part of me thought to ask him the details, as I would have before, but I was overwhelmingly convinced that I didn't need to anymore. I stayed silent, listening.

When the family he worked for moved from Salta back to Buenos Aires, Basilio followed. He worked as a doorman in Barracas, for a building filled with Syrian Jews. One of the residents, several years older than him, was named Alberto Julio Masri and served as the president of the Or Torah community in Barracas until his death in 1985. Don Julio, as he was known, was a jack of all trades: he dealt with divorces, liaised with the police commissary, and oversaw the operations of Hakham Suli's Hebrew school. "One day, they invited me to a brit milah at Or Torah," he told me, referencing the ritual Jewish circumcision. "I was very embarrassed. I didn't speak a word of Hebrew. I was the only non-Jew there! But I went anyway and got along very well with them all. I felt like I belonged." In the years that followed, he grew close with many members of the community.

Basilio worked with these people while they were still alive—first as a baker, then as a doorman—and ultimately ended up as the keeper of their graves. "My boss, who brought me here in the first place, is buried here, too." He spoke of some of them as his closest friends in the present tense—even though now, at eighty-six years old, he was just about the only one left. He said he'd watch over them until his own final days.

———

**Posted to Facebook group SI, YO FUI AL RABINO
ELIAS SULI DE BARRACAS (Yes, I Went to the
Rabbi Elías Suli School of Barracas)**

Jordan Salama
Good evening, all. My name is Jordan Salama,
I'm a writer in New York, from an Argentine family.
My grandfather, Moisés Salama, is in his nineties
and he also lives in NY. He was born in Barracas
in 1928 and still has very good memories of
the neighborhood and of Jajam Suli. He was
a good friend of the son of the rabbi, whose
name was Jacobo, or Jack. I am working on a
project now about the Syrian/Arab Jews (turcos)
in Argentina, especially those who worked as
traveling salesmen (hamleros) in the countryside,
such as my great-grandfather Selim Salama,
who sold fabrics with his horse-drawn cart along
the cordillera of the Andes between Mendoza
and the Bolivian border. If anyone by chance has
anecdotes about my family or similar stories, or
any other comments, please share them below!
My grandfather and I are very happy to be in
contact. Saludos para todos!

63 Comments
(a selection, translated from Spanish)

Diana Laham
A pleasure to meet you! I think I met your
grandfather! In my father's butcher shop! I am

the daughter of Yuque Laham and I was born two blocks from the temple!! All our grandparents who came from Syria knew one another, many in Barracas! Un saludo muy grande!

David Muhafra
Don't forget...one of the founders of the knis Or Torah was my grandfather David Muhafra, member number 26. That synagogue was made in the Sephardic Shami style, Syrian from Damascus...

Isaac Cohen Chaluh
Jordan Salama, a pleasure to read your note and see that you have so many wonderful memories of our neighborhood. As they say here, all our grandparents got off the boat and settled in the neighborhood. The love that we have for our ancestors, the respect we showed them, and the legacy they left us . . . so much humility, honor, and respect. We are relatives, come to think of it, and my father surely told me about your family. Les mando un fuerte abrazo.

David Freue
Hello, a pleasure. My grandfather was Selim Srour, an Arabic singer known artistically as Selim Ambram. We lived at 457 Patricios, and surely your grandfather knew him. I think that the Salamas lived half a block away from us... I remember all

this very well, considering that it's been close to forty years since I last lived in Barracas. Saludos a todos.

Adolfo Lati
I am Adolfo Lati. I was friends with your uncle Elías and I knew your grandfather Moisés. We called him El Negro. We lived on the same street, Brandsen. We were in the same high school and the same medical school. Un recuerdo grande a los dos Salama.

Ariel Suli
Hi, Jordan. My name is Ariel Suli. I'm from Barracas and my father z"l was called Mario, his brother was Jacobo [Jack Suli], who your grandfather knows... I would like it very much if you could ask your grandfather what he can tell me about my uncle, since they knew each other.

Silvia Pérez
My name is Silvia Hasbani. I'm from Barracas. I worked as a teacher for the Rabbi Elías Suli. And now I teach French in Buenos Aires. My grandfather was one of the traveling salesmen... and also one of the founders of the Sephardic community of the neighborhood. All the names and places that you mention ring loudly in my ears.

Buenos Aires

2020

I'VE ALWAYS BEEN COMFORTED BY THE SOUND OF murmurs in the morning, when you're still just half awake but far from the first one up. When you can faintly hear others having a quiet conversation in the kitchen, or down the hall. Perhaps you can hardly make out what they are saying, but just the fact that anyone is speaking at all is comforting—the security that someone might be there, looking out for you, even if you cannot see or exactly hear them. As one careens into adulthood this is one of the feelings that nobody prepares you to lose.

One warm summer morning in Buenos Aires, several years after my first wintry trek through the Andes, the voices murmuring in the kitchen were those of my abuelos. It was early, the low light glinting through the windows, the capital city rumbling to life. I was still in bed, and I could hear them in the other room of our rented apartment; suddenly I was transported back to their house in Peekskill, a child sleeping late after a long night of watching scary movies with my brothers and cousins, hearing their faint voices downstairs as they sipped mate in the stillness of morning.

I was in my twenties now, a college graduate trying to find my way as a writer who told stories about the world. Over the years that had elapsed since my return from the Andes I'd realized that it was precisely the histories of my family, the tales they passed down, that made me want to make a career of telling stories myself. I had written a skeletal chronicle of my journey up the spine of the cordillera, by land from Argentina into Bolivia, for a paper in school—sparingly recounting a trip that I at first considered to have been a failure. In those mountains, I did not find a single trace of concrete evidence showing that my great-grandfather, who died in 1960 at the age of seventy-four, had been there at all. Claudio Cruz Caqui wasn't his long-lost son, and Jorge Hanna's old book did not contain his name.

But I never did forget about my time in the Andes, nor my time in the capital during the weeks before and after that journey. When I came back home, I wanted to speak more Spanish, surprising my family when my use of the language featured the argentinismos that I'd learned at home with the Farfán Elías family in Campo Quijano, and with my cousins in Buenos Aires—or when I pulled out Arabic expressions like *oolee* and *ya haram* if something bad happened. Before, Spanish had not been part of the fabric of my existence, let alone Argentine "castellano." Now I sought it out everywhere I could. I turned one of my brothers on to drinking mate with me at home, without my grandparents around, and early on some Sunday mornings after playing soccer, I would drive alone to the corner of Junction Boulevard and Corona Avenue in Queens—where there is an Argentine bakery, a grill, and a grocery store that my grandparents and my father have long frequented—to buy yerba and medialunas and alfajores.

Certain things brought me, in an instant flash, back to Argentina. Not a day goes by when, heating water for mate in my little silver kettle and sipping it with a small gold-colored bombilla, I do not remember my time with the gaucho Pereira on the Península Valdés, or with Alberto Balaguer in the wooden lodge of Mendoza. I hear the sound of the bandoneon and I am transported to the classic café-bars of Buenos Aires; I look at the clay manka on my shelf and I recall the ancestral trade I made with two women in the breathless air of La Quiaca. There was a story to be found within every object, I realized: objects as simple as a narghile pipe or a book. I began to understand, if ever so slightly, what Abuela meant when she said that nostalgia could be, at once, so addictive and so devastating.

The fact that I was looking for something, anything, had been reason enough to introduce myself for the first time to members of our large extended family—our known family—which was scattered across countries and continents. We created a Facebook group and a WhatsApp chat called "Salamas por el mundo" that blew up with old photographs and conversations and memories. "Now, remind me again, you're the son of whom?" This was a question I answered over and over again. "And China y Negro are your . . . grandparents, alright." Sometimes this meant I could visit new places, and so I learned that one of the many virtues of being a Salama is that you have a place to stay—and family, no matter how distant, to take you in—wherever you go. I never tired of being a houseguest (though perhaps my hosts tired of me). Sometimes, on any given morning in New York, while tuned into an online Argentine radio station that played tangos and folklore, I thought about what these people might be doing. In Mexico City, I knew that my father's cousin Coco would awaken long before everyone else, at four in the morning, to post a "poem of the day" on Facebook. In Barcelona, my great-aunt Teresa, over one hundred years old, swam and used a stationary exercise bike. On the Florida and California coasts, my cousins Josh, Adam, and Rachel were preparing for their university exams, as were Dana and Martín and Sofi and Vicky and Maru in Buenos Aires. Also in Buenos Aires, scattered about the neighborhoods of the city, were an army of shopkeepers and salespeople who tirelessly made a business of selling ropa interior, undergarments, trying to understand why people were so particular about the only clothes they wore that most people would never see.

All of this had culminated, somehow, in a visit together: my abuelos, my father, and me. This trip was different from those of the past, when I hardly wanted to speak Spanish and didn't know my way around the city. I'd begun to plant the seeds of my own life in Argentina, too.

There is no better time to be in Buenos Aires than during the twilight of the austral summer, when the weather is pleasantly warm and the city seems spellbound beneath an eternal, golden glow. The balconies of apartment buildings are replete with sunbathers and tea-drinkers during the afternoons. At night the streets pulse with energy until well into the early-morning hours, plazas and vintage corner bars and open-air terraces packed with revelers of life and of joy. In the afternoons, with cousins and friends, we would lay out picnic blankets in the crowded Parque Centenario—edging out our space on the grass among the Zumba dancers and the weight-lifters and the kettle-corn vendors and the children's sing-along groups—and share mate and pastries and fruit until the sun went down. We went to free music festivals, rode bicycles down to the green shores of the murky Río de la Plata, ate dulce de leche ice cream speckled with dark-chocolate chips. We had long dinners in Nestor and Corina's house, with Dana and Martín, sitting around the kitchen table until long after the food was finished, swapping stories about our families and our lives and our shared histories. I expressed myself in a fluid Argentine Spanish now, albeit with an American accent that would likely never fade. And I felt at home—a different kind of home than the place where I was born and lived all my life, but home nonetheless.

This time, when I traveled with my abuelos, it seemed that for them both, explaining their own memories and lives in Argentina to me was far easier in Spanish than it was in English, like it was in front of the *Historia Antigua*, or beside Abuela's recipe book of tales. Now that I also knew many of the stories already, as we walked for miles and miles through the city, the streets leapt to life. There—the old presidential residence in the city center, Abuelo said, where he once entered to deliver a package. There—in the neighborhood of Flores, the house where Abuela was born; in Once, the corner where her father, Isaac Oss, sold pastries in the street; in Floresta, the sidewalk where she played hopscotch beside an old tree that had long since been cut down. "When I was a little girl, I used to hop from one end to the other," she said, pointing to a dirt square that was not more than two feet across, "and I thought I could fly."

The stories were suddenly more colorful than they ever were in English: richer with emotion, more nuanced, more clear but often still so marvelous that at times it all felt like a delusion, a bottomless barrel of anecdotes that could never fully be emptied. It occurred to me, just then, how lucky I was: for so many others, the desire to ask questions about one's family often comes too late, only after the guardians of the answers are all but gone. I had the vast privilege of speaking to my grandparents as both a grandson and as a journalist, digging into their lives far more than I would with any ordinary story. For this, to me, was anything but an ordinary story.

One day, we surprised Abuelo with tickets to see Boca Juniors play a league match against Atlético Tucumán at La Bombonera, the venerable blue-and-yellow soccer stadium in the neighborhood of the same name, where Abuelo, as a child living seven blocks away in Barracas, would accompany his older brothers for matches in the 1930s and 1940s. "That was back when the stadium was made of wood," he said. His last game was sometime around 1949, he thought, maybe even as long ago as 1942. "It's been over seventy years for sure."

Yet for those seventy years he hardly ever missed a game from afar, be it by radio or by television or by rotating carousel of pirated online streaming sites. Before I ever spoke even a word of Spanish, my initial, singular connection to Argentina was through soccer—my only currency in a culture at once foreign and familiar—and of course this was why. Written into the *Historia Antigua* were all kinds of stories about the sport. When Abuelo and his friends played their own games in the streets with a ball made from muslin stockings and handkerchiefs with knots tied at the ends. When Boca won the championship in 1935 and "Moisesito" and all the other little children received little engraved bronze medals that said "al pequeño hincha boquense" (to the little Boca fan). The names and the team lineups and the winners and runners-up from the happiest days of his boyhood.

"Ya haram, that was fútbol," Abuelo said, recalling all of this now, in his nineties in Buenos Aires, tears welling up in his eyes.

With Abuelo, my father, my cousin Martín, and Nestor, three generations, we piled into Nestor's small white Chevrolet and set off for the field. Nestor drove slowly once more, as he did that cool and rainy July morning in 2017 when he picked me up at the airport, now not because he wanted to tell me what was on his mind but because he was as focused on hearing my grandfather speak as I had been all those years with the *Historia Antigua*.

Abuelo gave him directions to the field from memory.

"Tío, I'm from here," Nestor protested.

"So am I," Abuelo smiled, continuing to excitedly guide us through several miles of winding city streets from Caballito to La Boca. When we got out of the car, he turned toward me. "This is my barrio," he said. We still had some time before the game to walk around. "I'd like to show you all a few things."

So we began a long walk down Brandsen Street, from the Plaza Colombia toward La Bombonera, a ten-block stretch that could be considered something of a pilgrimage in our family. There were stories everywhere we turned. By looking at the façade of each house, Abuelo could recall the names of the families who lived there eight decades earlier. There was the Santa Felicitas Catholic Church, which according to neighborhood lore, harbored secret underground tunnels that were built in the 1800s; nearby was another parish church, where the priest was known to have several lovers who came by under the guise of confession, and where the Jewish boys sold figs and olive branches to worshippers during Semana Santa. On another corner stood the Basque milkman. "In those days," Abuelo said, "all the Basques were milkmen." He grinned. Just like all the turcos were traveling salesmen.

Farther down the street was Or Torah, the Syrian synagogue where, Abuelo reminded us, he had his bar mitzvah and Selim Salama told him the "ancient history" for the first and only time; it was also where Hakham Suli presided over the neighborhood Shami community, and where Jacobo Cohen Hop collapsed while walking to pray. Or Torah was a formidable, Levantine-looking building of arched windows and arabesque embellishments with an onion-shaped cupola. Men in black hats and suits wandered in and out of the towering wooden doors. "Hakham Suli spoke in Arabic," Abuelo said. "It was practically our mother tongue, because at home our parents spoke Arabic, too. But we were ashamed of that, and so we responded in Spanish, which we learned in the streets."

He made sure we passed the Sociedad Luz, the public library around the corner where he began studying in earnest and became involved in the socialist movement. Now, we learned, it was home to a teachers' college called the Instituto Alfredo L. Palacios, named in honor of the senator who was

Abuelo's mentor. We stepped inside; the last time he'd been there was sometime in the 1950s. Though the old books that ran all along the walls now had cracked and faded covers, there were young people studying across long, creaky wooden tables. "Es igual, igual," Abuelo murmured in awe. Exactly the same as he had left it.

Other things were long gone. Their makeshift soccer field, a courtyard filled with palm trees that was across the street from Abuelo's childhood home, was now a parking garage. Indeed, the home itself, 1588 Brandsen—with its three stories and forty-three stairs and long corridors and bay windows— had been knocked down and replaced by a modern-looking brick chalet. But the house next door was still standing, in all of its old-world glory: made of stone, with tall wooden doors and windows encased by black floral cast-iron grating. This was the same house where, in the afternoons, the neighbors played the piano with those windows wide open, the melodies drifting out over the street for all to hear. A few blocks over, in La Boca, the tango conductor Juan de Dios Filiberto added to the chorus of sounds, rehearsing with his orchestra from the living room of his house. I thought of all those tango cassettes piled up in the basement and in the van in New York. It made sense, this, everything. As Abuelo's memories flowed, the sun was setting behind him, casting a warm glow over the Plaza Colombia, full at this hour now with the sound of children playing under the shade of the jacaranda trees.

The person who seemed most affected by all of this was Nestor. Nearly three years had passed since he picked me up from the airport that rainy day in July and told me not to go to the Andes. "Can you believe that was where Selim

Salama read the newspaper and made up those stories to all his friends?" he marveled now, as we passed that famous corner of Brandsen and Patricios, where the old Muhafra general store had long since been replaced by a hot dog stand.

"I owe you a bit of an apology," he told me. "For real, eh? All Tío Negro's stories, maybe they mean something after all . . ."

"Es todo harta." I grinned, repeating what had become a running joke between us.

"No, no, no," he said, putting his arm around my shoulders like he always did. I couldn't help but think that as he walked through these streets with Abuelo, Nestor's memory was with his own father, one of my grandfather's older brothers, who had died a few years before. "That's not what I'm saying. I don't know how true those stories actually were. But what matters more is that we're still repeating them now."

Walking to the game, a father and his son passed us by. The boy, who couldn't have been more than seven years old, wore the same vintage long-sleeved jersey that Abuelo carried in his hands. With every passing block, the stadium drew closer, and the streets were increasingly filled with fans sporting blue-and-yellow jerseys and the sound of chanting and drums. As we approached the first of several security checkpoints, caught up in a parade of supporters walking toward the stadium gates, I spotted a camera crew from TyC Sports—the network that produced *Fútbol de Primera*, the old highlights show that first introduced me to Argentine football from far away, all those years ago.

I walked up to the reporter, a young man about my age

named Julian Cotino. "My grandfather lives in New York," I said to him hurriedly, "and this is the first time he's been back to Boca in seventy-five years!"

Cotino waved over his crew and in seconds the lights were shining on Abuelo in the twilight, the cameras rolling so quickly that he hadn't even had time to change into his jersey. He appeared on-screen instead wearing a white Planet Fitness T-shirt that read, in English, THUMBS UP!, as his arms were halfway through the blue-and-yellow sleeves of the jersey at his waist. My father watched on proudly beside him.

"It must be pretty special for you to be back here," Cotino said, "remembering all this."

Abuelo thought for a moment, and then he shrugged, frugal as always with his words.

"It's like any other day," he said.

It was a strange response, and the interview ended not long after that. Perhaps, I figured, he couldn't hear the question over the noise of the crowds. But we moved on toward the stadium, which lit up the night.

Inside La Bombonera, the stands were replete with supporters, the stadium astoundingly bright and full. So this is what it's like, I thought to myself. At home, I'd amassed a collection of photographs that I'd taken over the past few years at stadiums around Argentina, all of them empty. In Mendoza, in the forest park, from high above the grounds of Godoy Cruz. From behind the fence of San Martín de San Juan. At dusk in the silent stands of Banfield—on the outskirts of Buenos Aires, just a few blocks from the cemetery where my ancestors rested in Lomas de Zamora—where I'd convinced a groundskeeper not unlike Basilio Rueda to unlock the gate because I'd come from far away, to visit the team I chose almost at random simply because I wanted to stake my claim.

Behind each of the two goals were the "popular" sections, multi-tiered standing-room-only concrete bleachers, where the most fanatical throngs of supporters welcomed the home team by launching colored smoke flares and jumping and singing in unison. Accompanied by an endless cacophony of drums, the songs continued throughout the entire match, interrupted only when Boca scored—twice—setting off delirious roars of happiness. As the game went on, the sky darkened, and a very large full moon rose above the field. The air grew chilly, but the night pulsed with warmth. It's a special thing, I thought then, to feel part of something—part of a community, a culture, anything bigger than yourself—even if in the smallest of ways. It is a feeling that you never want to forget.

To me, this didn't feel like "any other day." The reporter had seemed so puzzled when Abuelo suggested this, so quickly deflating the moment on camera, whether intentionally or not. We continued to joke about it inside the stadium, during the game. Only after some time did I consider why, in that clearly very emotional moment, he might have said what he said.

I recalled that one night around the time I started reading the *Historia Antigua*, I'd gone down to my grandparents' basement and found Abuelo working on one of his paintings. It was the most familiar one from his collection: that same scene of a Buenos Aires street corner with pastel-colored houses, cobblestone streets, and tall wooden doors. There were perhaps six different copies of it lying around or hanging up on the walls. Now I knew that it looked just like Barracas.

"Abuelo," I had asked him then, "Why did you paint this street so many times?"

"Every time I think back to it, I remember something differently," he said, shrugging nonchalantly then as he did on camera at the Boca game. "So I figured I might as well paint it that way."

For Abuelo, it seemed, memory was not something that weighed him down, nor was it something worthy of grand, sweeping events. Quite the opposite, actually: it was constant, ever-changing, and imperfect.

Memory was a way for him to travel among the places and the periods of his life every single day, through the most ordinary of rituals and objects—to glide through all the rich, wonderful details without worrying too much about their precise accuracy but rather paying great attention to how they made him feel.

In that way, Abuelo was on the streets of La Boca, remembering all this, every day of his life.

———

A while after that, Abuela asked if she could read me a story.

"Of course," I said.

She pulled out a piece of paper.

"I don't know why," she began, and I'm of course translating here, "but with each year that passes, I miss Argentina more. I spent my childhood there, though my family, my friends, my neighborhood are no longer. But I have memories, and memories never fade.

"I remember the things we did, the friends who have gone. I remember my house, my siblings, my parents. How we played football on the patio, or marbles on the waxed floor of the bedroom. How we spent Sundays glued to the radio listening to the games of River Plate. How the Arabic songs flowed from the record player and how my mother sang to them as she washed the dishes.

"Once, I told my grandson that nostalgia is the most painful feeling in the world, and it's the truth. While I can always return to Buenos Aires, while I can walk the streets of my youth, I know that nothing will ever be the same."

She paused.

"So maybe," she said, slowly now, "maybe I'm better off staying home, living only with my memories. At least those don't change. And with each passing day they grow grander in my mind."

———

The end of our time in Argentina together was fast approaching. In just two weeks, with Abuela and Abuelo, we covered a remarkable amount of ground. We'd driven to the coast, through verdant pampas of cattle and horses, and sat eating fried anchovies in old seaside restaurants. We'd visited the delta of the Río Paraná, near the town of Tigre, where Abuelo used to row crew. We'd held reunions with every relative we knew in the city and more, going as far as to seek out the

youngest descendants of each of the branches of my grandparents' siblings and aunts and uncles. A numerous bunch,
these newest generations introduced themselves deferentially
to my grandparents. They had all heard, from their parents
and grandparents, of my abuelos' house, and wished to someday visit themselves. "In *Peekskeell*," they said, pronouncing
the town's name in an Argentine-accented English that was
all too familiar to me, and yet still jarring to hear from these
strangers who were immediately strangers no more. "They
say you walk into that house and it's like Buenos Aires, so far
away." It was true; I'd begun to notice the same. My whole life,
I'd thought of so many things about that house—the style of
the smooth and shiny hardwood floors, the way the food was
laid out on the table, the parrilla grill that had been built decades ago into the outside of the chimney in the backyard—as
perfectly normal, second nature, for it was all I knew. But it
had now become clear to me that so much was in fact very
deliberately meant to evoke another place that was otherwise
distant in both space and spirit.

On my grandparents' last day in Buenos Aires, I brought
them to see María Cherro de Azar. It had become almost tradition for me to visit the historian during the waning days of
any given stay in the city, to put things into perspective. We
met in a large restaurant called Gratto, on the corner of Sal-
guero and Corrientes, in the Almagro section of Buenos Aires. María and Abuela sat across the table, exchanging stories
from the neighborhood where they grew up around the block
from one another. Their lives ran parallel; they had friends in
common, but they never met. Their most direct connection

212 ▷ JORDAN SALAMA

was that María remembered, as a little girl, buying baklawa from Abuela's father on the corner after school. "El Famoso Oss!" she said. "He was so loved. He was so loved!"

María turned to me. "You knew everyone in the neighborhood," she explained. "They all looked out for you."

"Oh, yes!" Abuela concurred. "The tram driver would stop in front of my house, where there wasn't even a stop! If I didn't show up one day or I was late, the next day he would ask if everything was okay."

"Your neighborhood gives you an identity," María said, "and that was ours. It was a big family."

As they spoke, I couldn't help but notice the similarities between the two women: María and Abuela were the same age, with husbands several years their senior. The women were from Aleppo, the men from Damascus. It was strange seeing them on opposite ends of the same table, speaking with the same cadences, the same accents, the same turns of phrase, even the same vocalized tones. It was as if I were looking at two versions of the same couple: the one that left Argentina, and the one that stayed. I got the sense that Abuela was thinking the same.

Afterward, María invited us to her home, a few blocks away in Caballito, because she wanted to have Abuelo and Abuela sit down for formal interviews. She was in the business of documenting, after all, and this was her world long before it ever became mine. My father offered to wait at the restaurant with Abuela, for she'd chosen not to come. "Not today, Jordan," Abuela said, pulling me aside. "It's too much for me."

The interview with Abuelo took place in the same small

living room where I'd first heard María's almost-prophetic wisdom about the turcos' wanderings in the Andes. Light from the late-afternoon sun came in at a slant through the window and the antique books watching over their exchange seemed to glow, as if alive and remembering along with them. Abuelo drew street schematics from memory and mentioned the last names of families that María knew intimately well. She always knew exactly what to say in response, how to keep the conversation flowing like an elegant dance, and her way of asking questions elicited long and detailed answers, for the traditions of the past were, for her, still the present. She wrote by hand in a looping Spanish calligraphy that almost looked like Arabic script, in a notebook that seemed to be filled with testimonies like this one.

The interview lasted for more than two hours, and neither participant seemed to tire of it. I sat there in rapt silence—dipping ka'ak cookies in a second and then a third cup of Turkish coffee that I sipped slowly—listening to the epic story that was unfolding in front of me. "The most important thing," María said to me when the interview was finished, "the most important thing is that everything is written down. Always remember that if you write something down, no one can erase it. Someday, many years from now, someone might want to know about our community, who we were and what we did. And we may be gone but the information will be there, forever." Perhaps, I thought, there is something about people who are so dedicated to the preservation of memories—always wanting to write in order to relive, recapture, remember—that keeps them going.

But time was, inevitably, running out. Abuelo and Abuela

needed to leave for the airport. It was a strange feeling: my Argentine grandparents would be returning to New York but I would be staying, for several weeks more, on my own in Argentina. Back at the restaurant, on the street corner, we said our goodbyes. "It's something very beautiful, isn't it?" Abuela said. "To feel at home in more places than one. It breaks you in half and it completes you, at the very same time." She asked me to bring back all the many used books she'd bought on the trip but could not fit into her suitcase. "You can read them after I'm done," she said, giving me a kiss on the cheek. "Allah ma'ak, querido."

"Chau, Jordan," Abuelo said, giving me a hug before pulling the car door shut. And then, rolling down the window, he added with a smile, "Escribí mucho."

In the Argentine dialect of Spanish, the words *escribí mucho* could mean "I wrote a lot," but also the command "Write a lot." Was he telling me that he'd written a lot about our time together? Or was he encouraging me to do so myself?

I didn't have time to ask. "Escribí mucho," Abuelo said again as the windows rolled up and the car pulled away.

January 2023

From: Moisés Salama
To: Jordan Salama
Subject: Re: "if you are curious"

Jordan,

I don't know how this happened, but today on the computer something came up that you wrote, the subject "if you are curious," with a few pages. I would like to read the whole thing. Do you have it printed out? Saludos.

Abuelo

EPILOGUE

IT WAS THANKSGIVING AGAIN, AND THERE WE WERE, at my grandparents' house in Peekskill. I had come downstairs to Abuelo's library to spend some time with the *Historia Antigua*.

I'd been thinking about how all that had happened might fit together. As I continued to tell my own story over the years, I learned that family libraries like the one that held the *Historia Antigua* are more common than one might expect, especially in Jewish households. They are very often rather simple stories of people moving from place to place and creating worlds along the way. Family historians, I realized, crave discovery within their families' pasts in order to learn more about themselves. Focusing on the exact year in which an ancestor was born, or the precise spelling of a surname in a time when records were not properly kept, mattered less to me now. It had become far more important to me to build out a family tree through the living stories that remained, such that a seemingly disparate family could be united once more.

In the other room of the basement, my younger cousin Ilan Moisés Salama, rightly named for his paternal grandfather, was kicking a soccer ball against the wood-paneled walls. With every shot, the room shook: Abuelo's paintings of 1930s Buenos Aires, of colorful La Boca and of the stone streets of Barracas, wobbled on the walls. The books and folders and binders lining his workshop trembled but stood strong.

Reaching for the *Historia Antigua*, I noticed that right beside it there was a new addition to the bookshelf. It was a blue binder, not nearly as thick, and it was labeled JORDAN – ARGENTINA. I took it out instead. Inside was what seemed to be the beginning of a new collection: some of my initial writings on my time in the Andes, which I'd shared with Abuelo, had been worked over with a pen—corrections made, notes added. "I want to start organizing things for you," Abuelo said when I asked him about it later, "so you can someday write it all down." There was a map of where I'd been in the provinces, the printout of a Facebook post written by Radio Valle Viejo in Catamarca about my interview on their show, and newspaper articles written about my search, among other papers. As I'd begun to write my own essays and stories for publications like *National Geographic* and *The New York Times* in the years that followed, he included those, too.

The first page in the binder was what looked to be an introduction to this new collection, written by Abuelo. This is how it began:

> *Everything begins with one story. Whether that story is true, one can never be sure, but as it gets passed from generation to generation, despite being somewhat distorted, there can be some truth. And then people live and people dream . . .*

A loud crash interrupted my reading. The soccer ball had hit a plastic paint bucket. "Golazooo," Ilan Moisés shouted, lifting his shirt over his head as he ran around in circles of celebration. My little cousin hardly spoke a word of Spanish, just like me when I was his age. But something was there: he mumbled gibberish words in the same cadence as the Argentine announcers on television; he wore the jerseys of obscure clubs like Ferro Carril Oeste, gifted to him by Argentine relatives visiting New York, because neither he nor his father could choose between Boca Juniors or River Plate. I smiled. This, surely, could not have been what Selim Salama had imagined for his descendants: that he would make a life in Argentina only for them to scatter again, across the Americas and beyond. I also wondered how he would've felt to hear that, all these years later, someone came looking for him. Maybe he would laugh at the fact that even after he was long dead he'd successfully taken me for a ride with his unabashed tales of train crashes and warplanes and illegitimate children. But something tells me that he wouldn't—even if not a single one of his stories was true at all. Because he, too, valued the spirit of the *Historia Antigua*, that ancient history that he told his children so that it, and they, wouldn't be lost.

At the start of Abuelo's written version of the family story, my grandfather referred to himself and his seven siblings as the "survivors" of a family upended by movement every two or three generations for the past five centuries. Quite literally, he meant that they survived the experience of being born, which in those days was far from certain. But now, after a few weeks roaming the Andes, several months in Buenos Aires, and many more years connecting digitally with family far and wide across the world, I have come to think of this in another way. I think back to *One Thousand and One Nights*, that timeless collection of Arabian fables, in which the princess Scheherazade faces imminent death at the hands of a ruthless king and tells story after story in order to save her own life. There are endless tangents leading in endless different directions, but everything, everything rests on each story being better than the last.

I went in search of old stories but ended up writing a new one; I'd first come to Argentina alone in search of the Lost Salamas, but what I'd found were very revealing traces of a family I knew I had all along. Now I look back on my travels and I see it: a collection of encounters that when strung together show, in real time, the construction of an identity.

Stories are currency for survival in a world where we are perpetually faced with the prospect of our demise. Our stories are embedded within the traditions we pick up across the journeys of our lives and the languages we carry with us in the soles of our shoes. They are the identities we create in worlds foreign and familiar, remembered now but forever at risk of being forgotten. And we trade in them as we move about the world because we know that long after our precise names and places inevitably fall away with the years, the stories we leave behind will form the mark of an existence.

Faced with the great library of our wandering family, I slipped the thin blue binder into its place.

Acknowledgments

This project passed through the hands of many crucial readers on its way to becoming a book. Andrew Blauner, agent extraordinaire, has been a tireless advocate of this and all my work since the day we first met, and I am honored and lucky to have him by my side. At Catapult, Megha Majumdar ensured that this book would exist, Summer Farah provided helpful feedback during its formation, and Dan López came aboard with enthusiasm and expertise to bring it all together and into the world. To all of them, I am enormously grateful.

At Princeton University, Christina Lee helped me find my voice as a writer while the research was still only beginning and has remained one of my most trusted mentors ever since. I will always be grateful to the Dale family, whose summer funding award made my first journey to the Andes possible, and to countless other members of the community who have supported my work both during and after my time as a student there.

Words are not sufficient to describe the admiration and gratitude I have for Ben Jacobson, who for the better part of seven years has spent more time than anyone else reading and rereading drafts of this story and serving as a thoughtful sounding board all along the way. Forever I will cherish our conversations and our friendship.

I wrote much of this book in its current form during several extended periods living and working in Buenos Aires. It is a very special thing to feel at home in more places than one, and I have my family, friends, and colleagues in Argentina to thank for welcoming me so warmly into their worlds. May we all open our doors to the strangers among us so that we shall be strangers no more.

This is a family story, and it is my immediate family—my parents, my brothers, my grandparents, my greatest supporters—for whom my love and appreciation is written into these pages and everything else I do. To all past, present, and future members of the Salamas por el mundo, this book is for you, so we will always remember.

Book Credits

Editor: Dan López
Editorial Assistant: Elizabeth Pankova
Jacket Designer: Gregg Kulick
Design Assistant: Victoria Maxfield
Publicist: Andrea Córdova
Production Editor: Laura Berry
Copy Editor: Elana Rosenthal
Proofreader: Iza Wojciechowska
Editorial Director: Dan Smetanka
Editor in Chief: Kendall Storey
Senior Managing Editor: Wah-Ming Chang
Production Manager: Olenka Burgess
Assistant Production Editor: tracy danes
Executive Director of Marketing: Rachel Fershleiser
Social Media Editor: Dustin Kurtz
Associate Marketing Manager: Kira Weiner
Marketing Assistant: Alyssa Lo
Director of Publicity: Megan Fishmann
Publicity Assistant: Vanessa Genao
Creative Director: Nicole Caputo
Contracts and Rights Associate: Miriam Vance
Sales and Marketing Associate: Katie Mantele
Publisher: Alyson Forbes

© Gastón Zilberman

JORDAN SALAMA is the author of the critically acclaimed travelogue *Every Day the River Changes*, named a Best Book of 2021 by *Kirkus Reviews* and a top new travel book by *The New York Times* as well as a Princeton University "Pre-Read." Focusing largely on culture and the environment in the Americas, his work appears regularly in *National Geographic*, *The New York Times*, *Smithsonian*, and other publications. He graduated from Princeton University in 2019 and is currently based in New York and Buenos Aires.